The custard stops at Hatfield

KENNY EVERETT

WILLOW BOOKS, COLLINS, ST JAMES'S PLACE, LONDON 1982

Willow Books
William Collins & Co Ltd
London · Glasgow · Sydney · Auckland
Toronto · Johannesburg

Everett, Kenny
The custard stops at Hatfield.
1. Everett, Kenny   2. Entertainers—Great Britain—Biography
I. Title
791'.092'4   PN2598.E

ISBN 0 00 218040 5

Made by Lennard Books
The Old School
Wheathampstead, Herts AL4 8AN

Editor Michael Leitch
Title page illustration by Ron Mercer
Designed by David Pocknell's Company Ltd
Production Reynolds Clark Associates Ltd
Printed and bound in Spain by
TONSA, San Sebastian
Dep. Legal: S. S. 357 -1982

CONTENTS

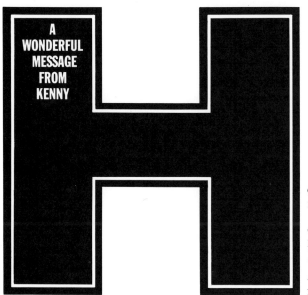

A WONDERFUL MESSAGE FROM KENNY

ello, darling reader!

Thank you for buying this book. You won't regret it. And neither will my bank manager.

As you will discover, what a truly amazing volume it is! If you place pages 16–48 in a pre-heated oven they will turn into a life-size replica of the Taj Mahal. Either that, or they'll burn a lot. But then, life's like that.

As you know, I've lived a quiet life, always eaten my greens and been kind to animals and TV chat-show hosts.

My ambition is to help old-age pensioners to build better motorways. (That bit was just in case my Mother reads this book.) For the real inside story of Cuddly Ken, look out – HERE COMES THE NEXT BIT!

THE
NEXT
BIT

SMALL AND SHAPED LIKE A HOT-WATER BOTTLE

from an ancient manuscript sent to Rome by a Governor of Judea, Publius Lentulus, in about 7 BC: 'He is tall and elegantly shaped; his hair falling in graceful curls, agreeably couching on his shoulders; his cheeks without blemish and of roseate hue, and his beard thick, reaching a little below his chin and parting in the middle.'

From an ancient manuscript sent to a filing cabinet by a registration clerk, Manny Handsmakelightwork, in about 1944 AD: 'He is small and shaped like a hot-water bottle; his hair falls like a premature Brillo pad; his cheeks look like a relief map of India and his thick tongue reaches a little below his teeth and dribbles a lot.'

The subject of the first description is Jesus Christ, with whom the subject of the second, me, has nothing in common except the birthday and the beard.

A Char Is Born!

The time: 3.00 am, 25th December 1944.

The place: Hereford Road, Crosby, near Liverpool. (*Too* near, if you ask me.)

The event: Much squealing, grunting, puffing and pushing.

The result: Maurice James Christopher Cole, later to become your own Cuddly Ken.

Four months later the Germans surrendered: draw your own conclusions.

I'm sure my Mother hasn't forgiven me for being born at that unearthly time of day. She used to take it out on me by showing me postcards of a place called Bootle which was near where we lived and was where you were sent if you were a naughty boy. Bootle was full of holes, due to the bombs and Hitler and all that.

If there hadn't been a war on I'd probably have been born in a hospital, but in those days hospitals were for pansies so I was born at home. Makes sense really when you remember that there were people with legs hanging off from the war. A birth was quite a normal thing: a bit like 'flu.

The First Memory!

Looking up from my cot and saying 'Moon'. (What was my cot doing out on the street at night?)

Hereford Road, Liverpool 21, is in between two sewage outlets from the River Mersey and the area was pock-marked with holes. I came into the world during the last dangling remnants of the war and the Germans had this thing about bombing. The docks were nearby and they used to come over and strafe the surrounding area. But they obviously couldn't be too accurate because they were going at a hell of a lick and when they passed over they just said: 'Right zen Fritz, lets drrop zem here,' and a lot of it fell around us.

Mum's name is Elizabeth. Her maiden name was Haugh and Dad used to

This chapter illustrated by Paul Leith.

call her 'Heave-Haugh' for a laugh. Humour was very thin on the ground in Liverpool.

Dad's called Tom and he was a tug-boat captain. He used to get the ships in and out of the harbour during the war. When he wasn't doing that he used to do naughty things to Mum and here I am: five-foot-three of wiry, white blancmange. I probably would have been built like Marble Arch if Mother hadn't been so bad at cooking. She knew more ways to murder an egg than any woman alive. Mind you, it wasn't entirely her fault: there was a war on – rationing and all that and she only had one little cooking ring, rather like a little camp-fire bunsen burner with little holes around it. I remember it used to go 'bang' a lot and we'd all dive under the kitchen table in case the Germans had decided to come back for a bit more of Bootle.

Our house was very, very thin and was part of one of those streets that looks as though it's all been thrown together by mistake and on the same day. It was a bit like a battery-farm for humans in the true Coronation Street tradition, and, to give you an idea of what it was like, they sold it recently for £3.50.

Basic, I think, is the best word to describe the house. The walls were thinner than paper and you could hear very clearly what was going on in the houses on either side. Mind you, in those days it didn't really matter because nobody had tellies or radios. All that broke through the plasterboard was the sound of the people next door having rows and opening tins of soup.

————————————— **Scarred For Life By A Bottle Of Lucozade!** —————————————

Oh yes, before I forget, I've got a sister as well: Kate. She's a year and a half older than me and she was really horrible when we were kids. She's great now, but when we were little she used to play evil tricks on me. She once peed into an empty Lucozade bottle and told me it was lemonade. Being a trusting soul, I drank it and it tasted delicious. Funny though, I've never been able to touch Lucozade since.

That was the sort of thing we'd do to amuse ourselves in Liverpool. There weren't any electronic video TV games, you see, so we peed into bottles while hanging around, waiting for someone to invent Space Invaders.

Kate and I used to sleep in the same bed. She would sleep with her head down at one end of the bed, by my feet, and I'd sleep the other way up, by hers. Cosy, huh? Not to mention smelly.

————————————— **Speaking Of Smells . . .** —————————————

Grandad (Mum's dad) lived in Bootle: just underneath a giant poster for 'Aunt Sally's Liquid Soap'. He used to smell of old-age and Gillette shaving soap and he used to bounce me up and down on his knee and call me 'Sundown'. As I said, there wasn't much to do in Liverpool.

Every other day Mum and I used to go and visit Gran. She used to smell of old-age and underwear, which helped when it came to telling the old folks apart.

She used to spoil me rotten like all good grandparents are supposed to. I'd get threepence for sweets, which would be like getting 50p these days, and the sweets were fab! Flying saucers made of paper with exploding sherbet inside that sent your tongue into a tiny paroxysm of delight . And liquorice. I remember always being encouraged to eat liquorice because they said it kept you 'regular'. Being 'regular' was the most important thing in the world in ye olde days. As soon as you got to school they'd cram great loads of prunes and figs down your gullet.

As you can tell already, mine was a charming family, especially Grandad who used to keep a spittoon lying around and he'd occasionally send whopping great missiles of flob hurtling around the house. Odd, really, a bit like having the loo in the lounge.

There wasn't exactly a lot of money around in those days but we weren't poor enough to qualify as 'picturesque', even though life was far from comfy. No mixer taps, Badedas, toasters or Thermawear for the bijou-Everett-ette. There were all the basic life-support systems, but none of the things we all take for granted these days. Our bathing system was a laff-a-minute. The bath was in the kitchen and there was a board on top which held the bread bin, the vegetables and all those kitcheny things, and when we needed a bath which was once a week we'd take all the stuff off the top of the board, heat up this cranky old geyser which dribbled about a millilitre a month and then all take it in turns to scrub off a week's worth of grime. Dad went first, of course, being bigger than the rest of us and then, in order of seniority, the other members of the family followed suit. It's just as well I didn't have a younger brother: he'd have been swallowed by the mud!

It must have been about then that I discovered a fool-proof method of gauging the temperature of bathwater: bum-dunking. If the water doesn't feel just right when you dip your bum in, it's in need of more hot or cold. Remember that folks – it comes in handy when you're making soup, too!

The Family Estate

. . . well, garden actually. Well, when I say garden, it was more like the size of this book. Not big enough to walk around.

You'd finish your stroll before you'd started it. But people used to have them because they were handy for dumping old bicycles.

We did have one bit of green in Liverpool. There was a field just across the main road, between our house and the beach. Beach! Well, it was really just where the River Mersey lapped against the shoreline. I used to count the bongies that got washed up: Durex to you. The beach was absolutely seething with millions of knotted bongies. I didn't discover what they were until much later in life, but counting them gave me something to do until I became a world-wide mega-star.

The shoreline around Liverpool was covered with unmentionable substances! The sewage would wash out to sea . . . and then come back again. That didn't matter a lot unless you lived in between two sewage outlets, like us. There was such a lot of gunk bobbing around on the water and on the beach that I used to have great fears that one day the world's oceans would just clog up. Someone, somewhere would pull one loo chain too many, and that would be it: all the ships would grind to a halt in a sea of smelly yuk. You can imagine how relieved I was to discover that most things eventually go back to their basic constituents and that the world is unlikely to sink just from an excessive weight of turds. Damn clever, all this nature stuff!

God Slot

We were a very religious family, extremely Catholic. We used to go to Mass every Sunday, and Confession once a week. I can't remember the first thing I ever confessed, but the biggest thing I ever owned up to was what they politely refer to as 'playing with yourself'. That was the next worse thing to murdering your granny. You can go to hell for ever if you die in the time between having a wank and getting into the Confession Box. Imagine! Going to hell for that! If God hadn't meant us to wank, he'd have put our bits and pieces somewhere where we couldn't reach them.

We were all terrified of God. They'd tell us frightening stories to keep us in line at school. 'God is always watching you,' they'd say, making him out to be some kind of beady-eyed spiritual Big Brother. 'He's everywhere,' they'd say, 'inside you, outside you, watching your every move.' I was frightened to fart in case I upset him.

I don't know how I had the courage to do the things I did with my first friend, Peter Terry. He lived around the corner from us and his Mother was a wild-eyed, Irish looney. His Dad was always walloping people and scowling at the world. How he managed to have such a jolly, likeable son as Peter I can't imagine. Peter was a real tearaway. We used to sneak through the back entry of Irwin's grocery store and pilfer tins of peaches which were the height of luxury. Then we'd have to lug the tins home with us because we didn't have the foresight to bring a tin-opener. We ended up going into the God business, Peter and I, but that's another story (of which more below).

Nowadays kids have inter-galactic guns and pinball machines to play with. We used to have to make do with what was around so we spent most of our years hanging off lamp-posts. They had gas lamps in those days, and there were two twirly sticks of iron with a blob at each end coming out of the top; we'd clamber up the posts and hang from the twirly sticks for hours on end, like a couple of bats. And, of course, we did all the usual things like skip, jump, throw balls, punch girls. Just like normal healthy boys are supposed to. If we were feeling really daring we'd work our way down the street, ringing doorbells and running away. Thrilling, huh?

Our neighbours were really delightful people, too. I remember shouting some rude words at a housewife in the street one day and, instead of saying 'Ooh how cheeky,' she came hurtling over and beat the living daylights out of me.

Is it any wonder I used to dream about running away to sea? When I was a bit older I used to go on Dad's tug. It was great. There'd be all this spray and salt in your hair and the smell of old sailors mixing with the pong of the bongies. It was just like real life – like FeelyAllRoundVision-ipoos. There was even something romantic about the whopping great engines on the tug: all pistons and tubes and steam, and a couple of blokes in the basement shovelling coal all day long.

When I was five I was taken to this thing called a school. Mother scooped me up one day and plonked me in this strange room with thirty other kids. I promptly burst into tears because I'd suddenly been dragged away from everything I knew. I couldn't see the point in it. It seemed to be an extremely unnecessary exercise. My first teacher at St Edmund's was Miss Emright, and my first memory of her was when she patted me on the head and said: 'There there, don't cry little boy . . . or we'll nail your knees to the blackboard.'

When I'd quietened down enough and stopped sobbing, she carried on with the lesson which was all about the poor people of Africa, and how we must all put a penny in this Sambo head. You probably don't remember them. They were just big, black heads and you'd put a penny in its hand, press a lever at the back and this great big golly would eat the penny. If you had one of those things in your house or school these days you'd be arrested for racial discrimination. I remember thinking: 'Black people? What's she talking about?' I'd never seen one. There just didn't seem to be any when I was a kid.

I was a very inquisitive child. Always asking questions about everything, because none of it seemed to make any sense, like school and God and christening. But nobody in Liverpool would explain things to you. I remember asking Mum one day: 'Where did I come from?' and she just said: 'I'll tell you when you're twenty-one.' She dodged around the issue and I got upset because I thought it was something I'd done, so I burst into tears.

I was eventually introduced to the wild and woolly world of sex by my father when I was about seven. He chucked this book on my bed called *What Every Young Boy Should Know*, and on the first page it said: 'What every young boy should know, as transcribed from the cylinders.' That confused me even more. The book was full of extraordinary things like: 'Young boys who play with themselves should be strapped down to the bed'. Can you imagine anything more designed to turn people into sado-masochistic freaks than reading that sort of advice while they're still in short trousers?

We didn't talk a lot, my parents and I. Not past a basic 'How are you, what's for dinner' level anyway. But I suppose there wasn't a lot to talk about, me being all shy and confused.

─────────────────────── **Stalag St Edmund's** ───────────────────────

When I'd finally got used to the idea that school was going to be a daily occurrence whether I liked it or not, I began to take in my surroundings – and what a shock that was!

I used to have lunch in the Dinner Centre. Now, I don't know if you know about Sparta, but it was a place years ago where they'd sort out the weaklings by leaving all the new-born boys out on a cold slab overnight: the ones that survived could go to war and the others just faded away. The Dinner Centre was our version of being left out on a slab. If you survived the prunes, the figs and the sago you were fit to drive a tug and go to war. It cost two and sixpence a week for this privilege. The lady who ran the Centre was a bit like Rosa Klebb. She used to thump you in the back for holding your fork in the wrong hand. I got flung out one day for holding my nose so I couldn't taste the food as it went down. As well as the Rosa Klebb/Attila the Hun dinner lady there was another, wobbly one called Miss Jelly (true!). I could never understand what either of them was doing in a job like that because they obviously both hated children.

The classrooms were very old with wooden benches in a sort of staircase arrangement – high at the back, going to low down at the front. And there was a roaring fire which made it all quite cosy. My favourite teacher was Mrs Robinson, a little white-haired lady who really knew how to deal with children. The day we changed from pencils to pens was a big day in my life. She handed out these sticks with a hole in one end, and then we were given these little metal projectiles which were the nibs. And ink! You had this little inkwell in your desk and the game was to flick blotting-paper pellets, doused in ink, at the girl in front. I'd make up this sort of inter-classroom ballistic missile and flick it. The blob itself would take off like a rocket and splange all over someone so far away they couldn't tell where it had come from and the ink from the pellet would shower all over the other kids, resulting in nasty glares and broken limbs in the playground later.

The big event of the week, when I wasn't hanging off a lamp-post, was the Saturday morning pictures at the Odeon. *Rocket Man* and *The Curse of the Crimson Ghost* and *Flash Gordon*. There were slides on the screen to begin with, showing pictures and the words of songs, and a high-pitched chorus of hundreds of kids all sang *Run Rabbit, Run* and *Cruising Down the River* and *Old Father Thames*. Then we'd have a serial, followed by the live appearance of the Odeon Manager who'd go on stage and get us to play games, like throwing balls into a bucket.

One of my early triumphs in front of an audience was in the Odeon skipping contest. I am, it must be revealed here, one of the world's great skippers, and I beat a girl who skipped 300 times, even though I only managed about 280. I was pronounced the victor because I was much younger, and a boy! Boys weren't supposed to be good at skipping. But can you imagine how boring it must have been for the audience? Two kids jumping over a bit of rope, holding up Flash Gordon. It's a wonder they didn't throttle us with our ropes.

My prize was a jigsaw puzzle. Quite a simple one really, it was a picture of the Canadian-Pacific Express – in two pieces. Going to the cinema cost sixpence a week, which was half my pocket money. The other tanner went on sweets. Occasionally the kids would save up to buy things like pea-shooters and there were many arrests at the Odeon when the management conducted lightning pea-shooter raids! We'd be frisked at the door and they'd confiscate all our offensive weapons, including rubber-bands! Then they'd hide them in the cash register until after the show and we'd have to reclaim them on our way out. But there was no way for the management to tell the pea-shooters apart, so the big kids would rush out first and we weedy little giblets would be left with all the crummy ones.

When I say weedy, by the way, I *mean* weedy. It was incredible that I lived at all. I was like a pogo-stick with hair on top. RicketsMan! I probably did have rickets, because the only things in those days which kept us from giving in to the laws of gravity were orange juice and Cow & Gate dried foods.

Being so feeble, I used to get picked on a lot. The other kids would read *Beano*, *Dandy* and *Topper*, and when they'd finished they'd need something else to amuse their prehistoric brains so they used to play this great game called 'Let's Mash the Weed', ie Me! But I had this secret weapon when it came to retaliating: I'd fix them with a beady eye, flex my bicep and simper. They just weren't up to a wingeing, cringing, crumbling heap of blubbing jelly, so they'd end up leaving me alone. It was a technique which stood me in good stead for years. I thought: 'If I fight back, it'll only prolong it and I've no chance of winning.' Anyway, I couldn't see the point of anything to do with violence. I get hurt more easily than bone china, probably due to the fact that my skin is very close to my bones. There's hardly any padding.

I did have another method of self-defence. It's called 'Make Friends With the Classroom Thug' and it never fails. I latched on to the Neanderthal thicko with the protruding eyebrow-bones. He was the sort who used to drag his hands behind him on the floor. I made a point of sitting next to him in class and feeding him sweets at a rate of one every three seconds in exchange for protection. I used to swap my sense of humour – which was fairly weak in those days, but amusing to Zog or whatever he was called (Fletcher, actually) – for a guaranteed safe passage through the school day. Clever, huh? That was probably the first time I got out of a sticky situation by being what the Press now calls 'wacky'. It was a lesson that was to come in very useful in later life. It's very handy being able to deflect unpleasantness by hiding behind a silly voice or a gag. Wouldn't it be a good idea if everyone behaved like that? Especially politicians.

I wasn't the greatest scholar in living memory. I'd tremble at the sight of an approaching Bamber Gascoigne in those days (who wouldn't!) unless he was going to ask me about geography. I enjoyed anything to do with somewhere that wasn't Liverpool and, as most of the world isn't Liverpool, I used to get quite interested in pictures of Canada, with lumberjacks walking on logs down the Mighty Yukon! The other reason I liked geography was the way our teacher joined her rr's up (like this: *rr*). Very trendy, I thought. It's funny what grabs your attention as a kid, isn't it?

I was – and still am – no good at maths. Kids have it cushy these days with calculators. I'd have given my left tit for one of those. I could never see the point of counting things up. The fact that they were there was enough to satisfy me. What's the point of knowing that there are more than three of anything? Or that 3+2=5? To my mind, 3+2 is 3+2 and there's and end of the matter, d'you hear? The fact that it's called Five doesn't make a bit of difference and has never interested me in the slightest. What use is that sort of thing to a disc-jockey? I think, if you want to be a DJ, the less education you get, the better – just look around you, folks!

Crash, Bang . . . Codswallop!

Ours was a fairly normal family with Dad as the ultimate nuclear deterrent. 'Just wait till your Dad gets home,' Mother would say if I was naughty . . . words which struck a chill into my doobries! I got thumped a bit at home but I expect I deserved it for asking all those questions.

There was no walloping at the infants' school – we were too young to do anything really heinously awful. But later on, at St Bede's Secondary Modern, they'd bring out the cane and that was horrendous. All that weight and viciousness concentrated into a stick. It hurt like hell. I used to prefer the strap because there was the same weight and force but spread over a wider area. It used to sting like billy-o just the same, and occasionally they'd do it on the back of your legs instead of on your bum. Apart from the fact that it hurt, I thought it was a lousy idea: it never stopped us from doing anything and just made me feel angry as well as sore.

The day would start with breakfast at home: cornflakes usually, but on special occasions there would be a mixture of eggs, tomatoes, salt and pepper all squidged together in a great wadge romantically called 'Mush'. At school they'd feed us the government-prescribed mass of protein and vitamins which kept us going until we'd get home for tea – potatoes and carrots and things like that. And custard. There was a lot of custard in those days. They call it cream down South. Up North it's yellower and thicker and tastes better than cream. Cream tastes posh but custard tastes homely. Custard stops at Hatfield.

After school, I'd potter about in the streets for a bit. We'd go to bed really early in those days because there wasn't much else to do. I'd often be in bed by 8.30 and I'd sleep as much as I could. I still love to sleep. The only thing which wakes me up is hunger: the need to survive and cram curries into myself.

Dad encouraged me for a while to take violin lessons which was all right by me, except when it came to Saturday mornings and I'd be practising while all the other kids trooped past the house on their way to Saturday-morning pictures. They were all off to wallow in the adventures of Flash Gordon while I was stuck inside making these terrible noises. That somewhat dampened my enthusiasm for the necessary hours required to do violin homework and, in the end, I copped out completely by paying my niece a shilling to scrape away at the strings behind a closed door while I crept off to the pictures with the rest of the gang. Of course, one day, Dad caught my niece pretending to be me and he was furious. He cancelled the lessons immediately in a fit of pique. I thought I'd been rather enterprising in a way, but he decided that sort of initiative was not to be encouraged; so goodbye, violin.

──────────────────────── **A Present For The Folks** ────────────────────────

Mum and Dad have moved from Hereford Road. Slightly to the left. Actually they're in a nice, comfy bungalow in Formby with slippers by the fire and Ovaltine in the slippers. . .just nice and happy together, pottering about the garden.

I see them occasionally. One day I decided to pop up on a surprise visit and drove about five gruelling hours up the M1, pulled into Primrose Close and was walking up the path when the lady next door popped her head out and told me that my parents had gone to Brighton for the day!!!

So she gave me the key and I went in to have a cup of tea and use the loo. Then, as one does in polite society, I pulled the chain. . .but nothing happened. They'd turned off the water and I had no idea how to turn it back on again. I wrote them a little note: 'Dear Mum and Dad, just popped up to say hello. I've left you a little present. Bye.' And then I drove all the way back.

I think they're quite pleased with the way things have turned out. They've got all the pictures of me on the TV, and various awards I won for this and that. In fact they've had scaffolding built in the living-room to accommodate them all. We get on a lot better now than we used to which is probably because I've come to understand what a little monster I was and why I used to get walloped regularly. Noel Coward once said: 'Certain women should be struck regularly, like gongs.' My parents must have thought he'd said 'children' rather than 'women'; anyway, they took his advice very seriously.

My sister's quite a hoot these days. Kate married the guy who makes shirts for Marks & Spencer, so she's got a nice big house in Wimbledon and now that she's shaken off her humble origins to a certain extent, she's desperate to get back to being common again, because she's realized that's where all the fun is.

She phoned me a few years ago and said: 'Evvy, I'm having a pot party. What does one do? What does one wear?'

Speaking of pot (which we shall do again a bit later), my first-ever attack of the hallucinatories was on a cycling trip to Wales. When we were kids, a friend and I did the whole thing, there and back, in a day. On the way back it got dark and cold and we got more and more hungry and tired and the last few miles were spent in a state of extreme wobbliness because we were so exhausted. Trees turned into cotton wool buds and we weaved our way along the roads in a complete state of delirium. The next time I tried anything like that, delirium came in a capsule, but more of that anon, gentle reader. (You *are* gentle, aren't you? I'd hate to be wasting this on a great Neanderthal yokel like the one we had at St Edmund's.)

I got much the same effect from my first cigarette as I did from the cycling trip. We used to go to the local swimming baths and one day, when I was a nipper, one of the guys said: 'Hey, try one of these,' and handed me a Capstan Full Strength which I lit up and inhaled deeply into my lungs. 'Wow!' I thought, 'now I understand what people see in these things.' Everything went woolly and fluffy and I floated about a bit before realizing that the woolly, fluffy feeling was a prelude to hours of retching and puking. I threw up all the way home and haven't touched a cigarette since. Every time I tried to put one to my lips, my brain would burst into a Hallelujah Chorus of alarm bells.

Considering everyone else thought it very cool to smoke in the Fifties, I think I did pretty well to resist the social pressures, especially at parties. If you can call them parties. A bunch of people in odd, ungainly clothes congregating in dark, stuffy rooms, drinking beer. And the clothes! The late Fifties was not a good time for design generally, but especially for the rag-trade. Women's party frocks were hideous beyond belief: the girls would all look like balloons tied at the waist. I think that was the attraction. They'd squeeze themselves into these waspy waist belts and pull tighter and tighter until they got to the last hole which pushed all their innards out on either side of the belt, so their boobs were filled with lungs and stuff and blew up like great melons with pounds of kidney and liver and stuff straining against the tits, trying to get out.

And for the blokes, things weren't much better: winklepicker shoes which

tortured your feet and mohair suits which tortured the eyes of everyone who looked at you. I couldn't understand the Teddy Boy thing either, especially that funny little duck's arse thing they do to their hair, covering it with shoe polish and brilliantine. Why would anyone want to do that to themselves? It's like sharpening your nose.

I used to think caftans were the thing to wear, all loose and flowy and easy to put on. But, of course, I'd have been lynched for wearing anything like that in Liverpool. That's another daft thing: nobody objected to people walking around in shoes which piled your toes on top of one another, and with mounds of white margarine in your hair, but if you'd trolled down Lime Street in a caftan – WALLOP!

And the girls at parties! I couldn't understand why these blokes were spending so much time and hard work chatting up a gaggle of giggling girls who never had anything interesting to say. I was rather a late developer in the naughty-bits department, and the fact that the lads might have had ulterior motives prolonging their patience never occurred to me. Parties weren't made any more fun for me by the fact that I didn't like drinking. I didn't enjoy the taste and all it did was make the floor bob about a bit. Why drink anything that's going to do that? No, no. . .the whole thing was very strange.

I Discover That There is Life After Liverpool

Nowadays the centre of most homes is the television set. When I was a kid it was the radio. It was an old Marconiphone with exotic names on the dial like Braemerhaven and Luxembourg. In those days the BBC was called Droitwich Nat., which was probably where the transmitter was. Our link with civilization was the Light Programme: crackling through the ether would come those educated, erudite voices being entertaining and diplomatic. I think it was in those days that I formed a desire to enter the wireless world. It was a miracle and I was entranced by the fact that a small, brown wooden box with a funny net opening at the front could sound like a person, or an orchestra, a steam-boat, a cymbal, a tuba. . .anything you wanted. It still astounds me that a little paper cone can produce any noise known to the human earhole. I'd sit mesmerized by whatever issued from the speaker and then, of course, the transmissions would end and I'd be back in drizzly old Liverpool.

Maybe I was too young in those days to think ahead to being part of that magic, but the radio was the most wonderful thing I'd come across so far. At night I'd listen to the adventures of *Dan Dare – Pilot of the Future* on Radio Luxembourg, which linked with the comic strip in *Eagle*. He'd wear a three-piece suit and tie in the spacecraft and the baddies were called Treens. They were covered from head-to-toe in bands of golden steel, like a sort of metal Thermawear. Their headquarters were on Venus. It was a great disappointment to me a while ago when the Voyager probe returned with pictures galore of rock. . .but no Treens! Life is filled with disillusionment, even now.

And *The Goon Show*! That was the highlight of the week, every Thursday everyone would congregate around the little magic box and sit glued to the silliness of Spike, Sellers, Secombe, Bentine and all the sound effects. There's nothing like it today, unless it's a special occasion like The Royal Wedding. Even *Dallas* doesn't have the same kind of pull because it's just one programme in a sea of other goodies. The Goons were just *it*!

We'd never listen to the Home Service (the old equivalent of Radio Four) because it was too pompous. The old Radio Three

(The Third Programme) was filled with obscure bits of classical stuff by people we'd never heard of (much as it is today, really). So the Light Programme was our staple diet. I used to love *Music While You Work* because I'd only hear it if I was ill and staying at home being pampered with luxuries like Ribena. *The Goon Show, Take It From Here*, *Dan Dare* and all the others created a world that was as far removed as possible from life in Liverpool. We knew what they looked like because they had their pictures published in the *Radio Times* (which was printed then on the same lavatory paper it is today). People like Jimmy Edwards and June Whitfield were the Terry Wogans and Michael Aspels of my youth. They were stars to be looked up to and revered. One of the great things about my job now is that I meet all the people I used to think were gods. Imagine, June Whitfield a god!

I still consider myself to be a newcomer to the radio business, even though I've been working in it for something like fifteen years. But as long as the old brigade are still around on TV and radio, I'll always feel like a beginner.

The early music shows on radio consisted of an announcer doing time-checks and introducing tunes. A typical bit would be something like '. . .and now, here's the Northern Dance Orchestra playing one of our old favourites, *Button Up Your Overcoat*. It's five to nine.' Wacky stuff, huh?

My fascination with the radio went as far as staring at it for hours, even when there were no programmes coming out, just trying to fathom how such a fabulous thing could possibly exist. Having a good programme on it was just a terrific bonus. Nowadays if people are watching TV, and there isn't a mega-tyre-squealing car-chase in colour every seven seconds, they get bored and switch over. But the early radio programmes were something to be savoured. *The Goon Show* was the talking point for a whole week until the next broadcast. 'Did you hear that bit when Eccles said so-and-so. . .and when Bluebottle did this?' Even today, if you listen to an old *Goon Show* it's still funny. Apart from all the daft bits, there were some really good lines. I've never been able to pinpoint just what was so funny about the Goons, but I suppose that would be a bit like dissecting your favourite pet to find out how it works.

My first gramophone was a little plastic toy I was given when I was ten. It had a yellow plastic turntable on a blue base with plastic cogs and a little handle. From it would issue such astounding tunes as *Mary Had a Little Lamb*. But I thought it was capable of better things, so I wrenched off the arm so it would take bigger records and I'd go to Rosie's junk shop to buy brand new classical records for threepence. I'd take them home, wet the end of my finger to rotate the turntable and, using my finger as the needle I'd get the thing going by hand, very nearly keeping to 78rpm. I'd spend hours, just sitting around playing records with my little finger. There was also a record of Laurence Olivier playing Hamlet which I didn't understand at all. I just loved the magic of a voice crooning out of a little plastic object. I probably wouldn't have been so fascinated by this gadget if there had been more to do and more to talk about, but you just didn't in our house. Like most families, I suppose, we'd only really talk to each other if something important was happening, like one of us exploded.

One day I wanted to wire up my own little radio station from the front room, which was only ever used for weddings and funerals, into the living-room where there would be a little speaker. I typed up a copy of my very own Radio Times for the day and my plan was to play records into the living-room. The only problem was that the audience went out for a walk in the yard. Hardly surprising: who'd want to listen to a bit of *Hamlet* followed by a symphony played at almost 78rpm? The family weren't even interested in real radio, let alone a bit of string and elastic in their own home.

Christmas

If your parents wanted to give you a thrill for Christmas, they'd give you an orange and a bit of knotted string. The festive highlight for me and Kate was the arrival each year of Auntie Sadie and Uncle Jack. They'd come in and give each of us a crisp pound note. Imagine! A whole pound! Think how many threepences there were in that. I used to carry it gingerly to the bedroom and pin it to the wall where I'd sit and stare at it for hours, imagining all the things I could buy. I'd do that for about a month and then turn it over and spend another few weeks ogling the B side. That's the great thing about pound notes, they've got two sides, and even when you're not spending them, they just sit there worth a whole pound! At least they used to in those days. I don't think they had invented inflation then. I'd memorize everything about those pound notes: the numbers, the pictures and then, when the thrill of looking at a particular one had worn off, there would be the thrill of spending it. I'd never save up for anything, just dribble it out on sweets and things for as long as possible. It had to last because it would be a whole year before the next one.

Christmas was magic. The incredible excitement of reaching down to the bottom of the bed with your feet and discovering a lumpy sock. You knew that on the other side of the bedclothes was your Christmas stocking. . .oh, that smell. . .it was filled with nectarines and apples and chocolates in a box shaped like a train or something. And then there'd be a big present like a Dan Dare hat and then there'd be this big sense of anti-climax because, no matter how great your presents were or how many there were, nothing could ever be as good as the build-up to Father Christmas's visit.

I remember sitting at the Christmas Day dinner table, hearing it groan with yum-yums, like mince pies and turkey and all that. It all seemed bigger and more luxurious than it was because I was small and, from where my eyes were positioned, just at table-height, there would be this panorama of jams and cakes and pies and goodies galore.

Another aunt, Lil, used to come visiting at Christmas. She was a Hokey Cokey expert and would sit at the piano playing out of tune while everyone else got pissed and wandered round the room, holding hands. Then all the grown-ups would go out to the pub leaving us kids at home. One year we decided to raid the sideboard where all the drinks were kept. We had one taste of each sort of booze. Wine, whisky, vodka, crème de menthe, brandy, port. . .we tried them all with the inevitable consequences. I had my head down the toilet most of that night and the day after too. I'd never felt so ill in my life and my sister Kate decided to take advantage of me while I was weak: she got me to admit that I'd played with my 'thingy'.

The following day she sneaked on me to Mum and I was hauled off to Confession. Picture this 12-year-old kid with a king-sized hangover saying: 'Bless me Father, for I have sinned. . . .' I was told to take my mind off such naughtiness by jumping up and down on the spot every time the desire came over me. I then had to say ten Hail Marys and three Our Fathers which further compounded the shame because, when you went out of the Confession Box to do your penance everyone watched to see how long you sat there. If you were there longer than it took to say three Hail Marys, it meant you'd done something really unmentionable. My answer to this was to pray very quickly. I got the Hail Marys down to about seven seconds.

As with everything else, nobody would talk about bodies or sex in our house. I was aware of something dangling between my legs, but when I asked what it was, my Mother would call it 'your baby tummy'. Father never referred to it at all and always closed the door when he went for a pee. I never saw my parents naked. It was regarded as unnatural, unless you were a member of a communist family!

I'm sure people up North don't 'do it' for fun. But then, according to the Catholic faith, you're only meant to 'do it' for procreation. Takes all sorts. . . .

I had a paper round when I was a kid. Twelve and sixpence a week was the pay from Mrs Sloan's shop for doing one round at 7.30 in the morning, one after school and one after tea.

By this time I'd started to save the odd bit of money and I saw an advert in the *Daily Mirror* which said: 'Record Your Own Voice. Baby's first words. Weddings, etc. . . This magnificent machine will delight you and your friends indefinitely. £13.11.9d. Guaranteed.' There was a phone number which we rang and a man came round. A very clever con-man, he was, and he didn't bring the machine we'd seen in the ad. but he 'just happened' to have a Phillips tape-recorder which was £35 and even better. He started recording us all talking about whether or not to buy it and, of course, when he played it back, everyone was flummoxed. It was just like the radio! I pleaded and produced enough savings to pay for the deposit and, shortly after that, I bought another, bigger, better machine which had loads of buttons, and with the two tape recorders I used to do little bijou show-ettes for a friend of mine, Alan Haslewood, who lived in the Wirral.

One of my greatest achievements at around this time was failing the 11-plus exam. It was all far too confusing for your Uncle Ken. Questions like 'Divide 42 by 6' (to which I wrote 'Why?') and 'What is the capital of the isosceles triangle?' I think my parents were a bit let-down, but had rather expected it in a way because I had this will-o'-the-wisp mind which flitted from one subject to another and they knew I wasn't cut out for great things in the examination department. If I'd passed the test I'd probably have been an accountant or something by now, instead of an extremely rich, famous radio and TV star – and you'd be a few quid better off through not having bought this book.

So it was off to St Bede's Secondary Modern in Crosby. It was a very modern building, full of practising thugs just discovering that they had useful things on the ends of their arms called knuckles which could help you if you wanted to get your way with small, lily-livered punies like moi.

Years later I went back to the school when I was doing a TV programme called *Nice Time*. The television people said: 'Let's do a show in which Kenny goes back to school in a Rolls Royce.' Back I went and there were the same set of teachers, all old and sad. I feel sorry for teachers. It's an end to progressing as a person when you become a teacher because you don't grow up with your pupils. As soon as you get to the end of teaching one lot, they're off and another bunch of embryo villains come lolloping in to take the mickey out of you. It's like rewinding the same horrible tape over and over again and never getting a replacement.

I didn't really have a lot of friends at school. I regarded the whole experience as a big waste of time. I'd learned everything I needed to learn without school, things like speaking, reading and writing and, as far as I was concerned, I was just unlucky to be forced to spend my days with a bunch of kids I couldn't stand and who probably couldn't stand me either. It was only later on when I was doing things of my own free will and mixing with others who'd chosen to do similar things, that I began to get actually matey with people.

And sport! That was the other great horror at St Bede's. Sport to me meant that I had to strip off in the cold, put on a silly pair of white shorts, show my knobbly, spindly knees to the world and get out of breath a lot – all with no fun attached! How daft can you get? I used to play football and things only if I was threatened with a bashing from the sports masters, but I think they saw my lack of interest fairly early on and left me alone after a while. I just didn't have the body for it. . .still don't really. And the brain's not too hot either. So what am I doing here?

──────────────── **Le Monde Est Mon Huître** ────────────────

To my great relief they abolished conscription shortly before I left school. It had been my great nightmare that I'd have to go into the army for two years, an experience I know I wouldn't have survived. For one thing you have to wear those grotty uniforms and I'm allergic to wool. I'd rather be shot than wear wool next to my skin: there's just no point in living if you're that uncomfortable. I'd been fired from the Cubs when I was eight because of my allergy. Dad had proudly encouraged me to join the Cubs so that I could shin up trees and go dib-dib-dib round camp-fires. He bought me all the gear and taught me how to tie knots, which was all quite fun until I aspired to become a Scout.

Scouts have to wear this hairy, woolly pullover and I remember getting very excited about the new uniform until I put it on: trousers first, which were fairly hairy, and then the pullover which I couldn't bear for more than ten seconds. I ripped it off instantly, feeling as though my chest was on fire, and rushed to the Scoutmaster to ask if I could be a Scout even if I didn't wear the uniform. 'You must be joking mate,' he said. 'That's the whole meaning of the word. You all look the same and that's that – no uniform, no Scout.'

So I went to Dad and explained that I couldn't be a Scout because I had artistic, delicate skin. You can imagine how that went down! Him a tugboat captain an' all. He got very upset but there was nothing for it. My semaphore days were over.

──────────────── **Big Moment Number Seven** ────────────────

The year: 1954. The event: television came to Hereford Road! Yippeee! The sheer excitement of seeing things going on in your own home like *The Railway Children* and *The Appleyards* and *The Grove Family*. Even though programmes in those days were black and white and very stilted, there was a hypnotic fascination about the box itself. I gazed at it much as I had gazed at the old radio.

Programmes started at about 5.00 with an hour for children. Then the set had a rest and resumed at seven. *Panorama* was on the first day our telly arrived and there was also a programme with Katie Boyle called *Quite Contrary* – she looks even younger now than she did then.

We were the second people in our road to get a set. The first family to get one had the whole street peering in through the crack in their curtains at a puppet called Mr Turnip on a programme called *Whirlygig*, starring Humphrey Lestocq.

Once again I was excited beyond belief to see another lifestyle going on. What was happening on the screen seemed to be more civilized, more genteel, more fun than anything I'd previously come across. It didn't make me desperate to run away from Liverpool. That thought didn't occur to me. I didn't realize there were other, better places, only that the people on TV and on the radio were displaying attitudes of education and sophistication that I'd never seen at first-hand. And using complicated words I'd not heard of, like. . .'marshmallow'. They looked like a bunch of people who had discovered a way of having fun that didn't involve getting drunk and punching others.

In America people are instilled with the idea that anything and everything is possible. Here, the first word you hear is 'No'. Nothing seems to be possible or attainable, particularly if you're from my kind of background. The thought of actually appearing on TV yourself was just unimaginable. It wasn't the sort of thing that happened to the likes of us. Television was for Them, all those rich Southerners. Our sort went on boats and into bakeries. I have a feeling the same attitude still exists among a lot of people; even though everyone sits glued to the stuff that pours out of television sets in every living-room in the land, to work in television is not considered a 'proper' job.

The highspot of the tellyviewing week was *The Grove Family* on Friday nights. It was an early soap opera, like *Crossroads* only without the excitement. The Groves were just A Family in A Street with a Grandma, Grandad, Mum and Dad and youngsters, all sitting round talking to each other in immortal scenes like this:

'Ooh, Gran, you are a one.'
'Well, I'm getting on now, you know.'
'Oh, come on, don't be silly.'
'Well, I can't get around like I used to.'
'Well, I'm going up the pub for a pint.'
'Ooh, can I come?'
'No, lad, you're too young.'
'I am *not*.'
'Well, I'll go to the foot of our stairs.'

Etc, etc, etc. Riveting stuff, what? But in those days it was wonderful. Certainly more boring than anything that went on in people's own homes, but everyone loved it. (In fact, the more I think about it, the more it seems like *Crossroads*.) And if that was the high spot, imagine what the lows were like!

―――――――――――――――――――――――― **Heaven Can Wait** ――――――――――――――――――――――――

I was pretty short on ambition when I was thirteen or so. The way I saw it, I would just get a job when the time came to leave school so that I could help support the family and not be on the dole, which was considered highly shameful. And that was all.

But while I was still serving my sentence at St Bede's, an opportunity to kill two cooks with one broth presented itself. I was, to say the least, keen to leave, and my parents were frantically trying to encourage me to find some interest which would stand me in good stead when it came to choosing a career.

Peter Terry, this friend of mine who lived around the corner from Hereford Road, suddenly got the vocational urge and came over all sort of Joan of Arc, which resulted in a visit from a priest. A short while later he went off to the St Peter Clavier Junior Missionary School in Stillington, just outside York. Which was all very well as far as he was concerned, but it left me, still in Liverpool, without my best friend.

Some weeks after he went off, he returned home for a visit, looking highly healthy and tanned, with a big beam decorating his face. I'd never seen anyone look that way before and asked him how come he seemed so happy.

'It's fantastic out there,' said Peter. 'Even though you've got to do all the compulsory bits like Confession and lots of prayers and lessons and stuff, the rest of the time you spend gallivanting around this lovely old country house, shinning up trees, catching moles and playing games all around acres and acres of lush fields and forests.'

That night I lay awake thinking about the fun Peter was having compared to the fun I was having. I thought: 'Right, I've got to get this "Urge" thing he keeps talking about.' I sat on the bed, turning my brain towards Godly thoughts and trying to feel some deep, spiritual sensation. But all I got was backache, so I thought: 'Well, in that case, I'll just have to fib a bit.'

I told my Mum that my soul had taken wings and all that sort of caboodle and she was ecstatic at the thought of her little Mo going into the priesthood. As far as she was concerned, it was either that or become a movie star and, as there was little hope of movies, she seized on my declaration of religious fervour.

She picked up the telephone (oh yes, we had a phone, one of those big black ceramic jobs with a silver metal dial; we weren't allowed to touch it, though, because she was frightened we'd get electric shocks). She called the Missionary School and they sent over a recruiting person to check me out. I must have put on a convincing show for him because a couple of weeks later Mother was sewing labels into all my clothes and I was packing my bags in preparation for the journey to Stillington.

I arrived at this beautiful old house on a day when the sun was dancing around the fields, making things look even more beautiful than I'd imagined. The house used to belong to one of Queen Victoria's Prime Ministers, Benjamin Disraeli (a good Catholic name), and it was filled with polite, gentle priests wandering around in black frocks with their noses buried in Bibles. The rest of the inmates were a little more boisterous, but I'd been used to noisy brats all my life.

We slept in a huge dormitory which contained about a hundred beds and I remember hating the business of getting up in the morning and going into the shower department: there were no doors, and no hot water! But the house itself was just like a movie set: staircases, balustrades and minstrel galleries, all made from mahogany and populated by priests gliding about like ghosts on roller skates.

It was right up my street. I loved it: the countryside, the house, and most of all the quiet. I've always wanted to be quiet, ever since I was very small – although you'd never guess from watching *Blankety-Blank*.

The days would begin at six with a cacophony of bells jangling all over the house. I'd crawl slowly out from the depths of my pit while the other ninety-nine in the dormitory scrabbled around, making beds and rushing into the freezing showers. Then two hundred legs would climb into one hundred pairs of short grey trousers and we'd file down to a little chapel in the basement which smelled of incense. There we'd do prayers and stuff and the Communion bits and pieces. Little thin wafers would be held under your nose on a silver tray and they'd pop one on your tongue which you were supposed to keep there while you returned to your pew and thought wonderful, holy thoughts until the wafer dissolved. The problem was that we were so hungry we'd chew them on the way back to the pews. The sound of people chewing bits of God echoed round the chapel.

Then there'd be a lesson read from the Bible, followed by breakfast which was a real high spot because by then all the taste (and there wasn't much) of the wafer had disappeared and even the porridge with salt which they served up in the Refectory tasted delicious. The people in charge weren't like the Dinner Centre ladies who'd punch you if you didn't eat every last morsel on your plate. The priests just figured that we'd eat what we were given when we were hungry enough, which seems sensible to me.

Oodles Of Doodles

Every night I'd have to go to Confession along with everyone else in order to cleanse my soul for the following morning's Communion. One of the first things I confessed was pinching stationery. I was a prolific doodler but there wasn't much to doodle on so I'd nick paper and envelopes and sit happily doodling away at all hours of day and night. The trouble with Confession was that you unburdened this list of sins, like kicking, punching, stationery-stealing, and impure thought-thinking to the same people who were in charge of the place, so you couldn't own up to anything too heinous or you'd be out on your ear.

It was at this school that I first realized I had a choice about the people I mixed with. Until then I'd been flung together with a bunch of people with whom I had nothing in common, but at the Missionary School we all had a common bond uniting us (at least on the surface) so there was more to talk about and I began to be selective about my friends. I remained good mates with Peter Terry and began to learn how to handle friendships with other people too, so it was quite a crucial stage in my development.

There was a separate building in which we did our straightforward schoolwork, maths and geography and all the usual things; then there would be acres and acres of religious instruction, which may sound boring if you're not particularly into God but after a while I got used to it. At least you're being taught how wonderful things were/are/can be, and a few months of that rub off and make you quite optimistic, as long as you don't question things too deeply. I had a ten-foot-tall, red-haired Irish mathematics teacher who didn't do any better in getting my logarithms to work than the teachers at St Edmund's. He was a great mountain of a man without one iota of a sense of humour. All he could talk about was maths and I used to imagine him and his wife practising long-division into the small hours of the night. Sport played quite a big part in the daily curriculum – for everyone, that is, except me. I used to skulk around the white lines when we were all supposed to be playing football. I'd try to keep out of the way, running as far away from the ball as possible while trying to look as though I was deeply involved in the game – no mean feat, I can assure you. I couldn't see the point in running anywhere that didn't have something sensational at the end to compensate for all the panting and cold knees. Running to the pictures made sense, but running after a ball which everyone else was chasing. . .what's the point?

—————————————————— **Hooray For Hollywood** ——————————————————

The best bit of all happened once a month when we'd troop into the games room where there was a billiards table. We'd all group round a projector which would flash onto the screen some sensational religious movie like *The Song of Bernadette* in which Jennifer Jones has a vision of the Virgin Mary at Lourdes. Everyone else thinks she's crazy and I remember crying profusely, watching her stare with a Hollywood gaze at this celestial vision which appeared, in true corny movie style: a chick in a blue frock (Linda Darnell) with rosary beads hanging all over the place and shafts of light emanating from the palms of her hands. I thought it was Jesus who had the holes in his hands; I couldn't understand why Mary had them too. Eventually, to try and convince the other villagers of what she's seen, Bernadette gathers them all around, saying that she's been told to dig a hole to find a well of holy water. She scrabbles around in the mud to no avail and, when everyone else has toddled off amid murmurs of 'Pack her off to the asylum,' a little trickle of water appears in the last moments of the film and the heavenly choir sing their hearts out. I loved it, cried for ages. That was definitely the high-point of my time at the Missionary School.

I developed a small sideline hobby-ette while I was there: I started up a little dark-room next to the dormitory where I would develop any photographs taken at the college. This was, of course, long before the days of instant Polaroid pictures which are developed and framed before anyone's even taken the photo. The great thrill was to rush the job through and show everyone something that had happened about an hour ago. I'd take great pride in this because it made me the centre of attention for half a second and was loosely connected with show business.

—————————————————— **Amazing Grace** ——————————————————

Naturally, the conversations revolved around religious stuff and, although I went along with the game, I still hadn't been gripped by anything approaching fervour. I recall being ill one day and lying in bed, in the dormitory which had an illuminated

Our Lady at one end. I decided to have a go at getting a bit of God into my soul, because I was worried that someone would start asking questions and I'd get found out for the fraud I was. So I figured I'd ask this statue of Our Lady to get off the wall and come and have a chat.

'Would you please nip over and show us a quick miracle? Otherwise I don't see how I'm going to ever believe in what you're all about.'

Funnily enough, nothing happened, which only served to confuse me even more, but I resolved the dilemma by deciding that everyone else was just as mixed up as me, and that everyone had equal doubts but were just keeping quiet about them. I also came to the conclusion that I was having quite a jolly time and would stick with it until something better came along. The whole place was geared to producing missionaries to toddle off and sort out Africa, and that was the course on which I was set. Meantime it was quite fun, being surrounded by hundreds of people all of whom were like Cliff Richard, sweet and jolly and filled with good thoughts.

Confession, I decided, was the cleverest con-trick of all. If you obeyed the rules, there was no way of misbehaving and not being found out, because everything had to be confessed to save you from eternal damnation. I was once almost flung out when Peter Terry and a few other of us naughties decided to raid the Vestry which was where they kept the wafers, which were called Hosts. They hadn't been injected with the holy blessings at that stage, so it wasn't sacrilegious but we were just so hungry and they were the only things available. Not very tasty, as I said, but at least it was food.

————————————— **The De-Frocking Of A DJ** —————————————

We then discovered where the priests kept the altar wine. Disraeli had had massive underground cellars built, like catacombs. We took a candle down into a dark passageway, expecting skulls and things to leap out at any moment. Every so often we came across hundreds of bottles of wine locked behind great gates and I found that, being thin and weedy, I could scrape through a little hole and pass out the bottles to my partners in crime.

There we sat, at the age of thirteen, swigging claret like it was going out of style, when suddenly we heard the echoing of footsteps coming down the passageway. The footsteps came closer. . .then passed by. . .then turned. . .then came back again. I think my heart was beating at about 46 decibels because discovery meant certain expulsion which meant back to Mum's cooking. Fortunately we weren't discovered but I came close to being sacked not long after for telling a joke:

'What's impossible? Jayne Mansfield falling on her face.'

Hardly the most naughty of jokes, but some swine ·sneaked that I was wandering around telling rude jokes and the Head went berserk, wrote letters to my Mum telling her what a bad influence I was. The silly thing was that I didn't understand what was so bad about it: I didn't know that tits were anything more special than an elbow or a knee – they were just another bit of the body as far as I was concerned.

Again I got away with my terrible crime, but, about a year after I'd arrived, I went home for the Christmas break where, along with a pile of cards and Yuletide greetings, was a letter from the Missionary School suggesting that I didn't return. I was clearly not cut out for the work, they said, and it would be better if I turned my aspirations elsewhere. . .anywhere! The parents were very disappointed – first the Scouts, now the Priesthood. Was I forever destined to wander lonely as a chocolate éclair?

Isn't it odd that parents can be happy for their child to become a priest, which means never having a family or getting married to the one you love? I suppose it's about as respectable as you can get, the next best thing to being a doctor, but, as things turned out, I was not destined to become a doctor of African souls.

I was upset on behalf of my parents: not for my own sake but they'd put a lot of money into sending me off to be an errand boy for the Almighty. And the other thing that I felt miffed about was that, during my year at the seminary, I'd been laughing up my sleeve at the poor sods back in Liverpool who were still struggling through the grime and broken limbs of St Bede's. Now, I'd have to go back and do at least another year at ordinary school. Horror!

None of my experiences and learning about religion lasted. In fact I more or less gave up on the whole thing while I was still at the St Peter Clavier School. I thought: 'If I don't believe in it, there's no point in forcing the issue. I've explored every avenue I can think of, asked for some kind of sign from above, and still I don't feel cut out for plunging headlong into a life of do-gooding selflessness in the name of the Lord, so I'd better potter off and do something else until I feel a real Urge.'

I couldn't bring myself to get really committed without proof, to which, of course, the standard argument is that tale about Doubting Thomas and 'Blessed is he that believes without getting a behind-the-scenes tour of heaven', and all that stuff which I don't hold much store for either. I don't believe God would say that, because you'd then have to point to Hare Krishna or someone and say: 'Look, he's telling me exactly the same things you are, so who am I supposed to follow? What have you got that he hasn't?'

So now I consider myself a freelance spirit. When it's all over and I'm taken to the great Turntable in the Sky, that's when I'll think about it properly.

I suppose my motivation for going into the whole thing in the first place, apart from being with my friend Peter, was partly insecurity, a yearning to be accepted and a hope that there'd be some blindingly clear explanation of all those questions you ask yourself over the eighteenth brandy like 'Where am I? What is all this? What am I for? Why is the sky blue? Why does Tony Blackburn crack such appalling gags?' And the easy way out is to assume God knew what he was doing when he plonked us all here.

To my mind, life is like a film, with the explanation coming at the end. There would be no point in having the explanation at the middle.

The possibility of reincarnation intrigues me. It seems reasonable that you can't learn everything in one lifetime so perhaps you do a lot of homework each lifetime and answer a lot of questions, getting more and more clued up about the whole thing as the eons pass by.

The best person to talk to God about is Cliff Richard. He doesn't say anything that gives you concrete proof, of course, but he leaves you with a rosy glow, giving off golden vibes and dragging his wallet behind him. He somehow manages to leave you better off than he found you, does our Cliff, and sprinkles a sort of Tinkerbelldust around your particles.

─────────────────── **Invasion Of The Luxemburgers** ───────────────────

When I got back to Liverpool, I found I'd missed out on a year of radio and hit records by people like Elvis, Bobby Rydell – and Cliff as well. I used to cycle round on my bike, delivering papers and singing along to his latest tune which was *I'm Looking out the Window*. These days we're quite good mates, in fact he's just phoned to ask if I'd do the backing vocals on his latest single – isn't that sweet?

That's the great thing about what I do now. I've met all the people I used to admire and accomplished almost all my early ambitions, like cycling to Wales and buying a typewriter. I had a dream about a typewriter once and decided I had to have one. Everyone else wanted flashy red sports cars: I just wanted to type. No wonder the priests kicked me out. This kid is weird!

It somehow seemed impossible to entertain thoughts of being rich and famous. Things like that belonged to a different set of people. Come to think of it, though, the possibility of being famous was not quite so unattainable if you thought of people like Arthur Askey and Ted Ray. They'd started in Liverpool and made it, proving to the rest of us that life had more to offer than scraping gunge off sausage rolls (see Next Bit but one). A lot of people ask if Liverpool is so ghastly that everyone works harder to get out, which is why the likes of The Beatles and Cilla Black and Jimmy Tarbuck have done so well. But I can't see that it's any worse than, say, Manchester or Hull. Perhaps it's the Irish influence, because there are a lot of Irish people around the area. Or perhaps it isn't. Perhaps the world's a Vesta Curry. . .we may never know!

I was, as you'll have gathered, a rather shy and serious child and it was only when I began to get an interest in radio and things technical that I found a tool to project myself. The little radio station I fixed up in the house had speakers all over the place and one day when Mum and Kate were sitting nattering away about the latest way to massacre steak, they suddenly heard Radio Luxembourg booming through the house and the announcer saying: 'And the winner of this week's star prize, that fabulous radiogram, is Catherine Cole. . . .' Mum went berserk, jumping up and down in the lounge. 'You've won, you've won,' she shrieked, 'a radiogram, how lovely!' Kate eventually calmed her down and explained that she hadn't even entered the competition, it was just me in the other room, mimicking the voice of the Radio Luxembourg announcer.

──────────────── **1001 Things To Do With An Electric Food-Mixer** ────────────────

I used to drive Mum mad with my endless fascination for taking machines to bits in order to discover how they worked. Time after time Mum or Dad would come back with some new kitchen gadget or a piece of machinery and within half an hour I'd have totally dismantled it, satisfied myself how the innards functioned, and got bored with it, leaving someone else to put it back together again.

Years later, when I was working in professional radio and trying to find ways of making new sound effects, I'd drive Lee, my wife, batty by pinching her food-mixer or coffee-grinder and setting it up in my studio at home so that I could pretend it was a spacecraft or the sound effect of someone having their bones crushed beneath a giant man-eating aspidistra.

I must have had a great deal of confidence in myself even at an early age (what happened to it later, I don't know darling) because according to Mum, when I was fifteen I scrawled 'BBC HERE I COME' all over one of her mirrors. I don't remember doing it and I've no idea what I used to write it with, but she says that she's only recently managed to scrape off the last remnants.

These days, Mum is a fairly harsh critic of what I do on radio or TV. She'd just seen the first of my TV shows for the BBC in which Cupid Stunt, the starlet who bores Parkinson to death, made her début. Mum disliked Cupid so much that I was given strict instructions to kill off the character. She liked my impersonation of Tony Benn, though, so I've kept her happy with that one at least.

When I joined the Pirates she wasn't worried about my safety on the ship, nor about whether I was getting enough to eat. Her main concern was how someone who threw up on a half-mile bus ride would fare during months on the ocean, bobbing up and down in a choppy North Sea. And, as we shall discover, how right she was. Mums know best.

──────────────── **What Not To Do When You Leave School** ────────────────

My first job was a great shock to me. I really wanted to pursue my lifetime's ambition to stay in bed, but that was not the way of the world. There was an advertisement in the local paper: 'Idiot wanted for smelly, sweaty, sausage-roll gunk-removing employment in grotty bakery. Crummy wages. Only berks need apply.'

Cooper's was the name of the company and the hours were 6.30am until about 5 in the evening, and my enviable task was to stand in between this very large industrial oven and the window. I joined the job in June. The sun was pouring in the window, the heat pouring out of the oven and there was your Uncle Ken, sleeves rolled up, a tender young epitome of delicacy, a star in the making, spending ten hours a day scraping off the dirty old fat that spilled out of the sausage rolls on to the trays. My pay was £7.10/– per week, which probably works out at about twopence a tray, or something criminal like that. I wouldn't touch one of those trays now for £1,000. But in those days there wasn't any alternative.

    My workmates were just delightful. One of them was a fascist heap of dung in human clothing who should have been shot at birth with a very large bullet with ragged edges. . .Grrrrr. . . . The memory of him makes me fume. He told me off because I made friends with Dolly, the chocolate-egg lady; I used to keep going into her department to scrounge bits of chocolate. One day this Neanderthal oik said: 'If I find you in 'ere again, I'll bash your bloody brains in.' So I thought: 'There must be more to life than this.' I stuck it for about two months and gave Mum about two-thirds of my wages. The rest I just frittered away on silly things because it wasn't enough money to do anything worthwhile with.

Things Begin To Look Up

To escape the bakery Yeti-man, I applied for a job in an advertising agency. To me it seemed like just an office job, but it was a spectacular change from what I'd been through. Douglas and Company took me on in their civilized office in Chapel Street, Liverpool. The place was filled with polite people in suits who laughed a lot and had fun, sauntering through their day's work. This was much more my sort of thing; I used to wrap up parcels and run round on errands for all the people in the building.

It was about this time that I first actually opened my eyes and ears and began to take stock of what was going on around me. The people in the office were pleasant and, when someone's nice to you, it's only natural to respond. Until then I'd been a clam, but suddenly people were talking to me in a friendly way and taking an interest in me. I wasn't just there under sufferance, because the law said I had to be. It was my own free will to work at Douglas and Company and mix with these nice, cheery people. There was a wonderful woman called Mrs Thayer, who's died since, I believe. She was like the Meg Mortimer of our office: a big, brassy, jolly lady who sort of took me under her wing. I remember crossing the road with her once and she said: 'Ooh, I must get some Bodymist and bacon,' and we both collapsed laughing. For some reason it just appealed to us, and it was good to discover that I wasn't the only one who laughed at daft things.

I bought a little moped thingy, an NSU Quickly, and I used to putt-putt the five miles from home to work every day, weaving in and out of the lorries. One thing about this struck me as a bit silly: the moped cost me about £60 and all my wages were spent paying off the machine I'd bought to get me to work in order to make money to pay off my moped which got me to work. . .and so on. I worked my way up through the proverbial ranks until I was a production assistant, which involved ordering the blocks for the ads in the papers and knowing what size screen for which paper or magazine, ordering people about and generally seeing that things got done.

One day the production manager told me he was going on holiday and asked me to take over while he was away. So I did the only thing a self-respecting coward could: I resigned. I knew that if the company were left in my hands it would sink without a trace amid a sea of Everett cock-ups. I just knew it was too much for little old me and I couldn't take the responsibility of seeing a company which had given me such a break and such a laugh go under because of my inefficiency.

Things Look Up Even More

Next step in the odyssey was to the *Journal of Commerce and Shipping Telegraph* where I spent my days impaling adverts on a big spike. It was while working there that my interest in putting bits of music and speech on a tape paid off. I used to make up little quarter-of-an-hour silly programme-ettes, sitting in my bedroom for hours, poring over my two tape machines, practising silly voices and learning how to match up one bit of nonsense with another. Jack Jackson was doing it on the radio at the time, and I learned a lot from him, but mine were a bit more looney and silly. I used to send them to a guy at *Tape Recording Magazine*, Alan Edward Beeby. He wrote a column for the magazine which I used to read and our correspondence began when I sent him a tape and he sent one back; tapes went back and forth like that for a while until one day he said: 'Why are you sending me these jolly tapes when you could be sending them somewhere which might do you a bit of good, like the BBC?'

I'd never thought of doing anything like that. I couldn't see how the BBC would be at all interested in the bedroom ramblings of a small Liverpudlian. But I figured it would be worth a try so I packaged one up and sent it off with a letter that went: 'Dear BBC, here's a little effort, waddya think?' Only not in quite such confident, polished words.

The tape consisted of a quick fanfare, me doing a few silly voices, bits of LPs, a Kennedy speech that I'd edited around so that it didn't make sense but sounded as though it should. . .all sorts of general daftness on a little reel which I sent off and promptly forgot about until. . .

. . .one morning I was about to climb on board my NSU to go to the office when suddenly a telegram arrived! Now, a telegram in Liverpool means only one thing: death. Nobody sends a telegram saying 'Hi, come to a party' because there aren't any parties. So the whole street gathered around as my quivering hands opened this message of gloom and doom and it said: 'Tape great. Come to London and be interviewed. Ring Wilfred de'Ath.'

──────────── **Yippee Hooray! Er, Fab Sensation!! Mega-Whoopiness!!!** ────────────

I remember driving along the Dock Road that morning on my way to work, holding the telegram in between my thumbs on the handlebars, reading it over and over and over again, missing lorries by millimetres. I was in a state of total euphoria, unable to believe that the BBC should not only bother to condescend to speak to me, but should send a telegram too! That morning I had my first feelings of 'what the hell am I doing working in this dump?' Such feelings were a little premature, so I suppressed them and wrote off to the BBC and said that I was looking forward to meeting them. They sent back details of trains and directions for getting there plus a map of Broadcasting House, and off I trundled. Mum and Dad were, of course, over the moon because here at last was an opportunity for me to do something they could talk about in polite company.

The train journey itself was a thrill: just being on the way to London – land of June Whitfield. When I arrived at the BBC my first impression was that it was like a giant cake. I'd never seen buildings so impressive before. Everyone was so pleasant, I couldn't believe it. The doorman told me where to go and then directed me to the office. People asked if I'd like a cup of tea, and then I met Wilfred de'Ath who told me I was a 'find' and was going to be a star. He took me home, showed me his wife, put her back in the cupboard and then poured me my first gin and tonic which tasted like perfume. (Very BBC drink, gin and tonic – they all drink G & Ts and wear Hush Puppies.)

I had dinner with Wilfred and his wife, and I remember him pointing out something that was on television about a 'pirate radio ship' called Radio Caroline sailing into a harbour somewhere. 'Interesting,' he said, 'but it'll never last.' I didn't know what he was talking about, I was so far gone on his gin, and anyway all I could see was a big boat with a stick on it.

I stayed in a hotel overnight, which was another thrill. The next day I woke up with my first-ever attack of show-biz butterflies, for that was the day of The Interview. I went back to Broadcasting House and gaped at the tape machines and piles of equipment everywhere. Then I was bundled into a studio where Ronald Fletcher was going to interview me, live! The clock's hands creaked towards the appointed time and suddenly there I was – everywhere. All over the country. I couldn't believe it. I thought: 'Hey, this is going out to places as far afield as Herne Bay, Ireland, Torquay. I've hit the Big Time!' Then he introduced me briefly and played three minutes of the tape I'd sent in called the *Maurice Cole Quarter of an Hour Show*. I sat listening to it again, hardly able to believe that it was happening. Mum would be listening, Dad, Kate, everyone I knew.

Then he asked me a few more questions, like: 'Are your parents connected with show business?' to which I replied: 'Oh no, they're all quite boring really.' My first radio *faux pas*, of which there were, of course, to be many many more.

When the interview was over and I'd come back down to earth I said to Wilfred: 'I'd love a job here. It's all carpeted and friendly and everyone calls everyone else Darling.' I was later to learn that 'Darling' is not necessarily a term of endearment because in anything to do with show business you meet about eight million people a day for about two seconds each and it becomes the biggest job in the world to remember everyone's name, so everyone instantly becomes 'Darling', or 'Dahling'. Anyway, Wilfred said that he'd try and get me an interview with Derek Chinnery who was (and still is) a big nob.

Then back I went to Grime City, and that could have been the end of it really. I'd had my big moment of pazzazz and fame, and I was quite content with that. If they'd called me and said: 'Sorry, dat's all folks,' I'd just have sunk back into the office routine. But. . . .

Things Look Up Further Still!

A couple of weeks later another telegram arrived telling me that I had an interview. I had to choose some records and work out a little spiel to do in front of Derek Chinnery. Back to London I went, but made the big mistake of having a drink or eight before the actual interview because I was so nervous. I staggered into this basement with an armful of records and Chinnery looked down his pince-nez at me and said: 'Ah, yes, you're this new wassaname chappie, aren't you? Well, here's the gramophone, here's me and there's you. Go.'

Needless to say I was exceedingly dreadful and I could see his reaction written all over his face: 'Damn time-wasting young whippersnapper. He's no bloody good. Might be in a while though, so we'll wait until he gets to retirement age like David Jacobs and see what happens.'

So that was that. I went out believing that I'd cocked up my golden opportunity. I'd met and failed to impress the Head of Everything That Is. But Wilfred advised me to send the *Maurice Cole Quarter of an Hour Show* to a Radio Luxembourg biggie called Morris Sellars who was involved in the early days of Pirate radio. He got the tape to the people who mattered and Blam! The very next day I was on a tender out to a ship. It was really that quick: rejected by the Beeb (a word, incidentally, which originated on the lips of the lovely Me) and off to the world of watery wireless.

THE SMILE ON YOUR DIAL

As so often happens in this silly business, I was in the right place at the right time. The Pirate ships were busy recruiting and I was a keen young lad, game for anything. The Radio London ship had just sailed in, having been kitted out in Texas with all the transmittery bits, and the people who ran it were on a desperate hunt for DJ flesh. They wanted to cash in on the action and money being made by Radio Caroline, which had come on the air a few months previously and had become instantly popular.

Much of the pop radio as we hear it today was pioneered in style and technique by the advent in the Sixties of the Pirates. Until Easter Sunday 1964, the BBC had apologetically played a quarter of an inch of a pop tune every twenty-eight years and then gone back to discussing gardening and recipes and playing Rostropovitch's Symphony in L. Simon Dee, who has now faded altogether from the scene, was the first Pirate voice heard in this country. 'Good morning ladies and gentlemen,' he said as he sat bobbing up and down on the ship named after President Kennedy's daughter. 'This is Radio Caroline, broadcasting on 199, your all-day music station.'

From the point of view of us DJs the whole thing was an exciting adventure with a plot by Enid Blyton. But from where sat the businessmen who ran the Pirate ships, the operation was big money and big business, run from Mayfair offices and funded by serious investors whose intention it was to make money. . .and have fun. A clutch of ships followed Caroline on the airwaves of England: Atlanta, Radio 390, Radio Invicta, Radio City, Radio 270, Radio Essex, Radio Scotland and Radio England who, on the evening the government announced their intention to rid the country of the Pirate pestilence, held a launch party at the London Hilton which cost £10,000. The optimism and flying-in-the-face-of-authoritiness made the Pirate period the most exciting and innovative period in British radio since Alexander Graham Bell invented the lightbulb.

Look at the programmes the BBC Light Programme were broadcasting in 1966. . .it makes you feel old. They had *Saturday Club*, with Brian Matthew. *Easy Beat*, described as a 'pop music show with the Johnny Howard Band, Laura Lee, Tony Steven, Danny Street, and featuring the BBC Top Tunes. . . .' Aaaargh! *Pop Inn*: 'a record rendezvous with discs and visiting guest stars and groups'. *Parade of the Pops*: 'a live lunchtime pop music show featuring Bob Miller and the Millermen, Vince Hill, Dougie Arthur, Tony Crane and other vocalists with guest stars'. Is it any wonder

This chapter illustrated by Peter Till.

that the combined audience for the Pirates was estimated at about 25 million? At least 23 million were just escaping from Vince Hill!

If you're a nostalgia freak, see how many names you recognize from Ye Olde Days of watery wireless: Roger Day, Brian Tylney, Phil Martin, Johnny Walker, Don Allen, Jerry Leighton, Jim Murphy, Tony Prince, Bob Stewart, Mike Ahern, Robbie Dale, Rick Dane, Rosko, Dave Lee Travis, Tom Lodge, Tom Edwards, Alan Clark, Phil Jay, Ian McRae, Eric Martin, Paul Kramer, Ed Moreno, Ron O'Quinn, Bill Berry, Chuck Blair, Boom Boom Brannigan, Larry Dean, Jerry Smithwick, Jack Curtiss, Dick Palmer, Guy Hamilton, Vince Allen, David Sinclair, Roger Scott, Mark West, Tony Windsor, Mike Lennox, Tony Blackburn, Dave Dennis, Chris Denning, Paul Kay, Mark Roman, Ed Stewart, Duncan Johnson, Keith Skues, Norman St John, Dave Cash, Noel Miller, Peter Bowman, Paul Burnett, Alex Dee, Dennis Straney, Andy Kirk, Hal Yorke, Leon Tippler, Peter James, Ted Allbeury, Stephen West, Edward Cole, Brian Cullingford, Mike Raven, Paul Beresford, Bob Spencer, Al Black, Stuart Henry, Tony Meehan, Jack McLaughlin, Mel Howard, Ben Healy, Drew Hamlyn. . .and more still. Where are they now? Many, of course, still work in radio, and some have disappeared altogether, but they all were members of the Wet Club which helped to style what comes out of your radio these days.

Eeeh, thems were grand ol' days. Especially when we were winning, and particularly with the sort of support we got from people. Take, for example, this interview printed in *Disc* in August 1966 with George Harrison who, remember, was at that point one of the four most influential people as far as the young were concerned:'I can't understand the Government's attitude over the Pirates. Why don't they make the BBC illegal as well – it doesn't give the public the service it wants, otherwise the Pirates wouldn't be here to fill the gap. The Government makes me sick. This is becoming a police state. They should leave the Pirates alone. At least they've had a go, which is more than the BBC has done. . . .'

Sweet old Auntie Beeb! When on 27th July 1967 the BBC Director of Radio, Frank Gillard, announced plans for a revamp of the old BBC radio networks into Radios One, Two, Three and Four, he also apparently said that the term 'sound broadcasting' had been discarded and that from that date only the term 'radio' would be used. In future, he would be known as Director of Radio and not Director of Sound Broadcasting. The BBC has, of course, livened up a bit since those days (not too much, just a bit) but it's interesting to notice that when they finally launched Radio One in September 1967, they took 14 DJs from the Pirates. Suddenly the *enfants terribles* of the airwaves became part of the Establishment. The early Radio One line-up was as follows: Tony Blackburn, Jimmy Young, Simon Dee, Stuart Henry, Me, Duncan Johnson, David Rider, Emperor Rosko, Dave Cash, Keith Fordyce, Denny Piercy, Ray Moore, Tony Hall, Pete Brady, David Symonds, Pete Myers, Bob Holness, Terry Wogan, Barry Alldis, Mike Lennox, Keith Skues, Jack Jackson, Chris Denning, Johnny Moran, Pete Murrary, Ed Stewart, Pete Drummond, Alan Freeman and Mike Raven.

At 7.00am on 30th September 1967 Tony Blackburn introduced the first-ever Radio One programme, beginning with *Flowers in the Rain* by The Move. The Press gave it a mixed welcome:

'. . .many listeners were appalled' (*Sunday Times*)

'. . .Auntie blew her mind today' (*Evening Standard*)

'. . .it was all go at Auntie's first freak-out' (*Observer*)

'. . .Auntie has lifted her skirt at last' (*Daily Express*)

'. . .as the sycophantic celebrations of young men whose talent lies in peddling adolescent dreams are part of a rather frenetic attempt to appear young, Fleet Street mainly welcomes the BBC's attempt to turn hip' (*The Guardian*).

What does that mean?

One of the most noticeable comments from listeners and Press alike was that Radio One appeared to be just like the Pirates, without the commercials. Ex-Pirate Screaming Lord Sutch said: 'The BBC have copied the best ideas from the illegal stations. They've turned out to be the biggest pirates of them all.'

These days there are popularity polls every eight minutes, but in the very first Radio One DJ popularity poll, conducted by the *Daily Mail*, Tony Blackburn was judged favourite DJ! The great British public just managed to redeem themselves in my eyes by voting me as Number Two.

When it came to my own opinions of Radio One, I found I had plenty to say, and not all of it flattering; but more of that anon.

───────────────── **Don't Read This Bit Before Lunch** ─────────────────

After all those eons of boring Light Programme music, listening to the Pirates was a revelation. It was all jolly and 'Hey, there's a pigeon on the mast, and here's another fab tune and it's really groovy.' That sounded more like what I thought radio should be – happy and bouncy. And there I was, suddenly, on my way out to one of these Pirate chappies on this little chug-chug tender. Exciting just isn't the word for it. I didn't even bother to tell the folks or the people I was working for that I wasn't coming back. It was like having been in prison for eighteen years and someone saying: 'Here's a hole in the wall. What do you think?' You wouldn't sit and think about it, would you? You'd do what I did. Vroooooooom!!

As I was on my way out to Radio London, thinking 'This is the life for me, sitting on a boat, bobbing up and down playing jolly tunes and telling jokes,' I suddenly became aware of this horrendous feeling deep within my soul. The feeling soon identified itself as 'Here comes the puke', and I was sick three times on the tender on the way out to the ship. When I arrived aboard the ex-American minesweeper they'd kitted out with a transmitter, it was tossing around on the North Sea like an egg-cup in the middle of a gale, and people were hoiking great sides of beef and pork into the chef's department. That smell, coupled with the overwhelming pong of diesel fuel and the non-stop swaying movement. . .well, I was a goner. For about two months I lay flat on my back, only getting out of the bunk to throw another cupful or two of yuk down the nearest loo. Or, in dire cases, over the nearest disc-jockey.

I was luminous. Green to the gills. It seemed to me that the ship was engaged in constant combat with the elements at all hours of night and day. Force Thirty-Six gales were swooping on us with a vengeance. The chef didn't bother to mix up food: he'd just leave it sitting around and let the weather be his Fanny Cradock.

For weeks I lay there looking longingly at the twinkling lights of Frinton, thinking that I'd give any part of me, or all of me, or anything that was left of me to be in Frinton. How many of you can say that you've ever longed for Frinton?

The first night was so bad that if the tender had come back I'd have jumped on it straight away, vowing never to set foot on another boat as long as I lived. I couldn't see any way I'd ever get over the dreadful feelings, and decided that I wasn't cut out for a life on the ocean wave.

Fortunately the tender company who used the ferry us DJs on and off the ship, along with the supplies, had a row with the management of Radio London and they stopped deliveries for about two months, during which time I was forced to find my sea-legs.

I didn't eat for weeks. I'd throw up at the mere mention of food, let alone the sight of it. And then one day one of our newsreaders, Paul Kay, said that I had to eat something or I was going to expire within hours. I was wasting away. My fingernails weighed more than the rest of me put together. So I agreed to try and force something down and he helped me to the Mess where I was greeted by the sight of a massive pile of pancakes and syrup!

The chef was, without doubt, a murderer who'd been taking lessons from Mum. He was Belgian and used to cook everything in sump oil. And there it was, my first real attempt at food in about two months. I tried. I did, honestly, but it got about as far as the Adam's apple, and then. . . .

Fortunately, while all this heaving was going on, the management and technical people were still puzzling over how to work the transmitter so that we could begin broadcasting. This gave us all a chance to get used to rocking about on board the ship. And we all had a chance to get used to each other as well, which was handy as nobody knew anybody else. As well as me, Mark Roman, Dave Cash, Earl Richmond, Paul Kay, Duncan Johnson, Tony Windsor, Mike Lennox, Chris Denning, Ed Stewart, Keith Skues and Dave Dennis were all preparing for a full-frontal attack on Caroline and the BBC.

Our ammunition included a package of jingles prepared by the American owners and recorded by the PAMS people who later did all the Radio One jingles. Nobody in England had heard anything like them before. 'Radio London, 266: the smile on your dial.' Corny now, but they were very professional and slick and we knew we were off to a flying start before we even got going. We knew we'd conquer the airwaves. As indeed we did. About six months later we had twice as many listeners as Caroline and we were streets ahead in the market we had set out to capture.

I remember my first show. It was Christmas Day, my birthday, when they first entrusted me with the airwaves. I turned on the microphone and said: 'Tonight I want you to get very, very, very drunk. Forget about all this don't-drink-and-drive stuff. I want you to get really plastered, so drunk that you'll be completely incapable of even finding your car!' Pretty good line for starting off with, I thought. The others were all listening on board and their faces were getting more and more worried as I extolled the virtues of getting blind drunk, but then I just saved the day at the last moment and made it all OK, so they relaxed and I carried on being daft and playing silly tunes.

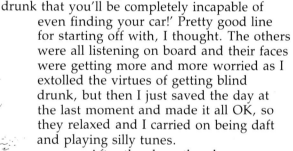

After the show they hung me over the side of the ship by my ankles. One of those old sea-faring customs which dates back centuries: after every record show from a boat, the disc-jockey has always been hung over the side. I went along with it. Always having been traditionalist.

How To Avoid Being Called Maurice

Up until Radio London I'd been plain old Maurice James Christopher Cole (Mum still calls me 'Our Mo'), but after I'd joined the Pirates our great big Texan programme controller, Ben Tony, a huge great beef of a man, came on board one day and told us that we all had to change our names for legal purposes. I've never been able to fathom out why, but I was always willing to oblige anyone who signed cheques. So I dug around in my brain cells for a good name. I think I'd just seen a movie with an actor called Edward Everett Horton. He was a star from the Twenties to the Forties, an American comic who made loads of films and later appeared on television as a Red Indian chief in *F Troop*. I quite liked the name Everett so that came first, followed straightaway by Kenny. Goodbye Maurice, 'ullo Ken. So, while my family still call me Maurice or Mo, my mates call me Ev or, more original still, Kenny. The Press call me 'whacky, zany, enfant terrible', and I'm not saying what I call them!

All the other guys changed their names as well, even if only slightly, like Dave Wish who is better known today as Dave Cash. In those days it was considered very hip to talk with an American accent and Dave, who was born somewhere like Harwich, spent about five minutes on the other side of the Atlantic taking a crash course in Being Groovy, and when he came back his accent had changed into the one you can hear on the airwaves of England today.

Technical Talk. . .And A Bit About Socks

The ship bobbed up and down around its anchor three miles out to sea in no-man's land, beyond British waters. Things were forever flying all over the place: in the galley, in the rest-rooms and even in the studios. When the tender chugged alongside to deliver food and water, they'd throw ropes on board our ship and then they would hoik supplies aboard amid much banging and shoving which would ricochet down to the studio and send the records and jingles hurtling everywhere. Whoever was on the air at the time would then have to launch into a silly explanation about what was going wrong, which got rather unfunny after the first ninety-six times it happened.

We all shared little cabins which were on a long corridor off the main playroom where we spent our free time. I shared with Dave Dennis, who was great most of the time unless he was in a bad mood when he was like Hiroshima coupled with Nagasaki and chips! He used to have terrible sock problems and in the middle of the night I'd sense a great green mist oozing up my nostrils, just like the Bisto Kid. The problem was that there were no washing facilities on board so there would be regular emergency parcels of socks and fish fingers delivered by the tender company.

A tiny black-and-white television in the playroom was the focal point of entertainment when people weren't working. Reception on board wasn't very good because the ship kept circling around its anchor, so the aerial was constantly veering away from the transmitter on land. We rigged up a handle which was linked to the aerial on the mast, and whoever was sitting nearest had to keep turning the handle in order to keep it pointing at the transmitter which was about 10 miles away. There were times when our transmitter, which was 50,000 Watts, would get in the way of the TV transmitter, and whoever was broadcasting from the ship would break through onto our telly speaker. This didn't matter much when there was a record playing because records are compressed and don't have any peaky, volumey bits, unlike the human voice which does, and this can be very annoying if you're glued to something exciting on the box. One day Ed Stewart and I were watching a concert on the TV, Schumann's Piano Concerto in something-or-other. We were riveted by this bit of culture in the middle of a sea of 45s and chatty drivel and suddenly Tony Blackburn's voice started to break through over the beautiful music. His inane babble didn't mix wonderfully well with the softness of the piano concerto so Ed decided to take his career in his hands. 'I can't take much more of this,' he said. He went down to the transmitter room and turned Tony down. The power of Radio London's output was drastically reduced for the length of Schumann's piano concerto, and nobody in London could pick up Tony's programme. Sorry, Tone.

─────────────────────────── **More About Tone** ───────────────────────────

The day Tony Blackburn joined us from Radio Caroline, all the guys were sitting around in the Mess, playing cards and reading dirty magazines, when Tony suddenly burst in and said: 'I'm going to be the best, most famous DJ in the world one day' and walked out again. How strange, we all thought. Still, if it makes him happy. Anyway, he's done all right, has our Tone, and good luck to him.

My only objection is that he claims he hardly remembers me from the Pirate days! Moi, who was to make such a massive impression on the world of entertainment, revolutionizing the English language as we know it today and contributing hugely to world peace. Can I have been such an insignificant little toad when I was a young man? Apparently.

'I hardly remember you on the Pirates,' said Tony, when asked recently about my fabulous career. Mega-cheek! According to him I spent most of my time asleep and his only clear memory of me on Radio London is when he saved me from death by drowning.

I've no recollection of this tale at all but, if the fiendish Blackburn is to be believed, he came across me one day when I was trolling about the deck of the boat, about to try and walk on water. He says that I was tripping on LSD and I was all set to emulate Jesus Christ's most spectacular stunt. He, so he says, grabbed me by the arm and asked me what on earth I was doing. I said that I was Jesus and was about to have a crack at natural water-skiing. Being the kind-hearted great big lummock that he is, Tony then led me gently by the arm and locked me in my cabin until the effects of the naughty substance had worn off.

Before Tony joined us on Radio London he, along with the rest of the

Caroliners, were in great awe of our station because of a clever little trick invented by one of our American gurus. No-one from Caroline was allowed on board Radio London, otherwise they would discover our great secret! The secret which made us more fabulous and famous and successful than they were. Actually, it was all a load of baloney, but after a while the Radio London Secret became enshrined in legend and on fag-packets, at least as far as the other Pirates were concerned, and some sort of mystical aura surrounded our station which was the envy of all others!

Yesterday's Orgasm

One day Brian Epstein, The Beatles' manager, who had quite a soft spot for us naughty nauticals, sent a copy of the latest Beatles LP, *Revolver*. It arrived when Ed Stewart was on the air. He played *Yesterday,* and while it was on, he said to me: 'Oh, just listen to this. Doesn't it just make you want to orgasm?' 'What a nice juicy word,' I thought. 'I wonder what it means.' When I went on the air, I played *Yesterday* again and said: 'Isn't that lovely, and do you know, every time Ed Stewart hears it, he has an orgasm.'

It was only when I went to Head Office a while later that I was told what it meant! They were molto crosso with me, until they discovered I didn't know what I was talking about. All was then forgiven except that in future I was forbidden to use any word during a broadcast unless I was sure of the meaning. If I didn't know the meaning of a new word I had to ask one of the bosses what it meant and then, if it was 'airworthy', I was given clearance.

How To Shift A Shifty Chef

The chef, as I've said, was definitely a homicidal maniac with a grudge against disc-jockeys. Things got so bad that we had to go on bended knees to Head Office, pleading for them to arrange to send a whole mass of Bird's Eye Dinners For One. Anything was better than the gunk dished up by the succession of cooks who appeared on board, each one worse than the last, culminating in a big Scottish oaf whose idea of enticing you to sample his wares was to shout: 'Shut up and eat the fucking stuff.' One day he had a violent row with Tony Windsor about something of massive importance, like boiled eggs. The chef pulled knives out of thin air and there was a frantic scene in the Mess as we crinkly little DJs tried to dodge this psychopathic pranny. I leapt fearlessly into the breach and flung a bottle of Heineken at the Scot who promptly turned his marauding attentions on me. Dozens of arms and legs were flying everywhere until eventually things calmed down and the shifty chef was bundled on to the next tender and probably dumped somewhere in the frozen waters of the North Sea.

How To Be Wacky

The programmes consisted of lots and lots of records, interspersed with wacky natterings and time-checks, and ads and about ten seconds of news every hour. Anything that got in the way of tunes was considered bad news. We were only a tiny outfit, of course, by comparison with the BBC, and we had no news-gathering facilities so we used to monitor the Beeb's news bulletins, change a word here or there, cross out anything that was difficult to pronounce and read it ourselves five minutes later in a breathless voice that was supposed to sound as though its owner had just rushed in from a massively busy nerve-centre. The Beeb got wise to this one day and added a phoney item of news to their bulletin just to see if we were silly enough to use it. Which, needless to say, we were.

I also carried on with my habit of knocking out those silly tapes and bits and pieces with which I pepper my radio shows to this very day. At least, on the ship, it gave me something to do instead of watching TV. I would record little jingles and promotions for other people's shows and the techniques I used were much the same as those I'd learned from my first two old tape recorders in Hereford Road. The added excitement this time was knowing that whatever I put together would be going out over the wireless waves in a matter of moments and heard by countless thousands of people.

It's a fairly nerve-racking business, waffling on the wireless. We were all very jumpy just before going on the air from Radio London, and even now, more than fifteen years later, I still feel a bundle of butterflies just before going on. There isn't a thing I do on television or radio which doesn't play havoc with my doobries. In fact, even on Radio Two, which is the most sedate, not to say asleep, radio station in the world, where nobody would even notice if you didn't arrive, let alone if you fluffed a word – even before going on Radio Two every Saturday my little frame fills with panic and, about ten seconds before I'm due on the air, I let out a custard-curdling scream which goes some way to waking up my producer and helps put some pep into my veins so that I can function properly and don't sound like any old person in the street. The last thing any old person in the street wants to hear on the radio is any other old person trying to sound clever. You've got to make them believe that you're clever to begin with, even though, of course, you're basically another old person in the street, except in a radio station. Did that make any sense? If so, please send £5 at once to the home for retired disc-jockeys.

A War Of Nurds

Those of us on Radio London were in deadly competition, of course, with the other Pirates, like Caroline and the others which were stuck on rigs left over from the war. People generally tended to leave us alone because we were quite well-established, but there were boarding parties and fires and mysterious goings-on on the other ships. Radio Caroline used to run aground regularly and we'd pretend to sympathize while sniggering behind our hands because they couldn't go back on the air until they unstuck themselves and got back outside the three-mile limit.

The Government didn't like us a bit and, in an attempt to get rid of us, they cooked up all sorts of stories like we were interfering with heart machines and kidney machines and police radio wavelengths. They also said that there wasn't enough room on the medium waveband for all of us. That was at a time when there were only a few stations on the air. Now how many local outfits are there? Tell me that, dammit! Perhaps they've suddenly found some more airwaves or something. We had very much the same trouble as the Citizen's Band people did until quite recently.

Initially I was paid £15 per week, which was quite good money at the time. Then people started to write in, the bosses realized that there were a quite a few people out there who liked me, and they put my wages up gradually, rising to £30 to £50 and finally to £150 a week, which these days would probably be worth £1,000! The work rota gave us two weeks on and then a week off. The biggest challenge was to spend all our money in the few days we had on shore. There was no tax to pay because the company headquarters were in the Bahamas, and there was nothing to save for. We were all too young to know the meaning of the word mortgage or anything like that. The only one who saved was Dave Cash and he bought a Bentley. Flash git!

It was dream salary time. Imagine being paid all that money for sitting on a boat playing records and saying things like 'That was Status Quo, wasn't it great? And now here's Sandie Shaw.' Beats working, huh?

We were entirely dependent on the tender company for our supplies of everything, including water. From time to time the tender people would have a row about bills or something with the Head Office and they'd stop sending anything out to the ship. The first thing to run out was the water and we were forced to conserve water for drinking, which meant there was nothing to wash in. As time went by we all got very smelly and grubby and we'd spend a lot of time avoiding each other as far as possible. (It's funny how you don't notice your own pong, only that of others around you.) Eventually even the drinking water ran out and we resorted to gallons of Heineken, which is not too great for making tea with.

In the middle of the Mess there was a drinking fountain which had long dried up but we were convinced that somewhere, lurking at the bottom, there might be at least a cupful of the much sought-after elixir. We undid the bolts of the drinking machine, ripping at it like a pack of wild animals and there, in this rusty, grey tray at the bottom, was a little dribble of a puddle of a smidgen of a droplet of water which we cut into slivers and each had half a thimbleful, savouring the oily, rusty taste as though it were Dom Perignon.

The crisis worsened, and it was obvious that the Big Wheels in their comfy London office didn't appreciate the horror we were living through. 'What do they need water for? They're bobbing about on top of millions of gallons of the stuff.' One of the guys, Paul Kay, went on the air and said: 'Ladies and gentlemen, I'm afraid we'll be going off the air tomorrow because we've completely run out of water; we all smell like the north end of a south-bound vulture and our throats are parched dry for lack of the stuff. The only course of action open to us is to switch off the transmitter and drink the water which cools its valves and stops it from blowing up.' Naturally, as soon as Head Office heard of this plan – which would mean the station coming off the air and thereby lousing up their advertising revenue – there was, surprise, surprise, a tender full of water whizzing out to save us.

The enthusiasm of those early days was something I'll never forget. I know it sounds corny, but there really was a sense of pioneering adventure about the whole thing. The money angle was important to those who ran the station, but even they and the advertising bods who looked after the revenue were really excited about what was going on. And the response from the public was sensational. There was hardly a radio in the South East that was tuned to the BBC: everyone had their ears glued to the Pirates, waiting for the next outrageous joke or the latest hit record which it would take the Beeb months to play.

The whole time was definitely a windmill, or is it a watershed, a sort of mini-renaissance. The tunes were greater than anything that had gone before, Mary Quant was revolutionizing the way people looked, LSD was changing the way people viewed things (as least we thought so then). Everything was geared to the young people of the time. We ruled the world and anyone over twenty-five was as good as geriatrified. And, of course, The Beatles. We were very instrumental in setting fire to their success because they were very 'Us' and we pushed their records as hard as possible. Everything clicked together like a giant jigsaw puzzle.

This was all going on in about 1965 and 1966, and '66 turned out to be my best year to date.

—— **The Best Thing Which Has Ever Happened In The History Of The Universe** ——
The Beatles were Yellow Submarining and Paperback Writing all over the place and were nearing the zenith of their popularity. One day they were playing a concert and a member of the audience threw a jelly baby at Ringo who, to the delight of the fans and manufacturers of jelly babies, stopped playing his drums, leaned over and ate the jelly baby. The next time the Fab Four appeared in concert, the air was thick with thousands of jelly babies hurtling through the air. Bassetts, purveyors of fine jelly babies since 1342, decided it would be a great idea to send one of the Pirate DJs to cover The Beatles' American tour and report back on how the jelly-baby-loving Mop-Tops were faring across the Atlantic.

At about this time I'd taken a small flat in Lower Sloane Street in Chelsea, and this was where I stayed when I wasn't on the ship. When I say small, I mean small: the kitchen used to fold into the lounge and the lounge used to fold into an envelope. I was lying in this envelope-sized flatlet one night when Alan Keen, Radio London's Programme Director, phoned me and asked the dumbest question I'd heard to date.

'Hi,' he said, 'how would you like to meet The Beatles?'

The Fab Four were, of course, my idols and I'd have given my right arm just to kiss the hem of John's socks. I'd have given any part of my anatomy, or any part of *anybody else's* anatomy, to scrape Paul's dandruff off his collar.

Then Alan said: 'I'm afraid you'll have to go to America with them, follow them around to about twenty different cities and spend a few weeks nattering to them about the tour and life and anything else they want to tell you.'

Can you imagine anything more blissful than going to the States, free, first-class, and trolling around the country with your idols? No, neither could I. It's like being told you've just won the pools *and* you're going to heaven to spend it.

─────────────── **Magical Mystery Tour** ───────────────

I packed my toothbrush and my Thermawear (getting a lot of plugs, Thermawear – where's my free set of undies?) and rushed on the plane. I remember hearing this thick Liverpudlian accent out of the corner of my ear: 'Which wun's Kenny Everutt?' It was Paul! Saying *my* name with his own lips! This mega-star of mammoth proportions, more famous than Max Bygraves, was acknowledging my humble, grovelling presence, not only on this earth, but on the same plane!!

I was a bundle of jelly-like quivering nerves at the prospect of spending a lot of time with The Beatles because I was only too well aware of my shortcomings. I had shortcomings stretching in every direction, as far as the eye could see. Especially when it came to interviewing; I was the absolute pits, dear! I would dangle a microphone under the nose of whichever Beatle I was talking to. . .and wait for him to say something. I hadn't worked out that interviewing involved asking questions which needed answering. I thought they did all the work and that witticisms and great sentences oozed like poetry out of their gobs.

My main problem was that the lads really weren't interested in telling people anything. They just wanted to play their music and get on with living. Questions were an invasion, especially naff questions like the ones I eventually came up with, and if you didn't ask a new question in a highly entertaining manner, you were spurned. I was very lucky because they knew they were trapped with me for the whole tour and so they took pity on me and let me get away with a level of incompetence which makes Monty Modlyn look like Sir Robin Day.

On the plane on the way over to America were the lads and their entourage, the Ronettes and Bobby Hebb (remember *Sunny*?). We were taxiing towards take-off in the middle of a thunderstorm at which point one of the engines went Kapflutblam! and blew up. The Ronettes promptly got off the plane, fearing for their lives.

The remaining band of intrepid aviators, myself included, sat pinned to our seats by fear and, as we finally took off, I remember John Lennon was gripping the seat for dear life; you could have read a book by the light glowing from his knuckles. I didn't really worry about anything. My only thought was: 'I'm going to die with The Beatles!'

─────────────── **With A Little Help From My Friends** ───────────────

My brief from Bassetts was to relay back to London a daily report and interview with The Beatles on how the tour was going. Which would have been OK, had it not been for my gross incompetence as an interviewer. The lads were friendly towards me, but I kept messing things up by asking dumb questions like: 'How's it going then, John?' What can a poor guy answer to that, apart from, as he did: 'You're not a very good interviewer are you, Ken?'

I would then suffer Hiroshima-sized attacks of paranoia and wander into a corner, feeling bad for days. Paul saw all this going on and took pity on me, thank God. He took me into the bathroom of the hotel we were staying at and said: 'Why don't you just ask me one question and I'll rabbit on for ages. Then you'll have enough material for ages.' Which was a godsend, because he gave me an hour's worth of tape which, by careful rationing, I was able to spin out to a few minutes' worth every day for the duration of the tour. What a sweetie he is! I pretended that I'd done an interview with him every day during the tour, but was actually just letting about ten seconds out every day, thereby saving my Bassetts bacon.

The system for relaying the interviews back to London for broadcasting was not exactly the height of space-age technology. I'd go to the concerts, hold the microphone up in the air and tape the sounds of the boys singing *Baby's in Black*, or whatever, along with the sound effects of a million knicker-wetting teenage girls. I'd then do a bit of colour commentary over the screaming hubbub and rush to the hotel to ring Paul Kay in Harwich. While he held a telephone earpiece up to the microphone at his end, I played a tape down the telephone from the other side of the Atlantic. He'd then take the tapes out to the ship on the noonday ferry, edit all the different bits of concert, Paul's interview and advertisements for jelly babies into a half-hour of totally inaudible, incomprehensible crackleness. The fact that you could hardly hear what I was saying didn't seem to matter all that much because the excitement of hearing The Beatles was what mattered, and the fact that the crackles were at least from America. Nowadays you'd never get away with it, because if every broadcast isn't in colour, nobody wants to know.

America's daunting when you first go there, especially if you're young and weedy and don't know your arse from your elbow. I was lucky that there really wasn't too much time to think about things because we were all carried through by the madness and sheer lunacy of the whole experience. The tour was incredibly well organized, which was just as well if you considered the possibilities which lay everywhere for disaster if one end of the arrangements didn't fit perfectly with the rest. There was an army of people whose job it was to do nothing but make sure that things got done.

It was all planned like a military operation right down to an intelligence network which one day got wind of the fact that a band of fans were planning to ambush the fleet of limousines which were transporting The Beatles and their entourage away from Shea Stadium. We stopped in the middle of a dark highway just outside New York and the organizers radiophoned Wells Fargo and asked for a big armoured truck to be parked about a mile away from where the ambush was due to take place. The limos drove on a bit and we were all told to schlep out and jump aboard a big cage on wheels which rumbled past the army of fans, all of whom were expecting limousines and waved the truck through without a second thought.

——————————————————— **Help!** ———————————————————

Philadelphia was nearly a disastrous stop for the tour. The group were giving a concert at the Rosebowl which is a giant, oval football pitch, seating about ten million times the number that can cram into Wembley.

I was with the Fab Four in the middle of the stadium, in a caravan, waiting for the concert to begin. The first rows of audience were way back, behind lots of grass about a quarter of a mile away from the stage and the whole area was alive with millions of kids screaming and stamping their feet hysterically. The madness escalated as the concert began and the music was totally inaudible above the wall of screams that came from the crowd. It was all very impressive and awesome and highly spectacular until one fan took it into her head to bust through the police cordon which was dotted along the border between the audience and the pitch.

The police, of course, hadn't really experienced anything like the heights of hysteria which were gripping the crowd and hadn't, seemingly, formulated a plan for how to cope with a runaway Beatlemaniac. So hundreds of policemen rushed forward to yank back this Yank, with the obvious result that the thousands of other fans were able to surge forward like the Charge of the Light Brigade multiplied by ten thousand. From where we were it looked like the Atlantic Ocean converging on this little stage – quite the most terrifying sight imaginable. The lads dropped their **guitars and hurtled back to the caravan which was instantly engulfed in the** sea of out-of-control teenagers and rocked all over the place, sending everything flying in all directions. We all thought we were going to die, but there was obviously nothing we could do about it so we jostled around inside the caravan, waiting to meet St Peter. Somehow the police managed to control the crowd eventually and we escaped by the skin of our teeth.

The four lads were just as scared as me, of course, but they'd seen it all before, only not perhaps at such a high-pitched level. At the beginning, when the mania business was just beginning, it must have seemed like the biggest joke in the world: all these kids going bananas every time one of them picked his nose. By this stage, however, they were too aware of the danger of the situation to feel anything other than pure fear.

The press conferences they gave were a delight. The reporters and cameramen would jostle with each other for the best position and they'd ask what were supposed to be searching questions only to be repulsed by the sarcasm with which the lads surrounded themselves as a form of protection.

'How did you find America, John?'

'We turned left at Iceland.'

That sort of stuff helped keep them from going mad at having to answer the same banal questions over and over again. They were also quite blasé, and **suspicious of people's motives in wanting to associate with them:** everyone seemed to have ulterior motives in being friendly, like wanting an interview, or an autograph, or a leg.

─────────────────────── **Daytripper** ───────────────────────

There was a bit of pot floating around on the tour, I seem to recall, and probably the odd acid trip going on as well, but I didn't really understand anything about it at that stage in my life. I remember Paul talking about LSD and saying how great it was. I nodded furiously, desperately trying to ingratiate myself with him and appear to be a hip, groovy swinger. But I didn't understand a word he was saying. I doubt if there was a lot of heavy druggery going on, because the schedule was so hectic there wasn't time for people to wander around claiming to be a multi-coloured fillet of haddock. When you have a druggy binge, you have to allocate a few days after it in order for your body to get used to functioning normally again. (I wasn't to get involved with naughty substances until a while later.)

─────────────────────── **I Wanna Hold Your Hand** ───────────────────────

Everyone in the States was desperate to get autographs. Everywhere we went there was a sea of bits of paper being thrust under our noses, accompanied by screaming pleas for us to ask the guys to sign their names. One day I just happened to have a ten-dollar bill in my pocket which I asked them all to sign, and the next person who asked me for their autographs went into multiple orgasm when I casually said: 'Sure thing, honey' and gave it to her. It's probably languishing somewhere at the bottom of an American drawer now, worth a fortune.

Until very recently I always kept my the Offical Beatles' Tour Pass 1966, with my photograph on it, in my wallet. It was a great memento but totally usless at the time. When the tour was in Canada I wandered outside the stadium for a moment or two to have a look at Toronto, decided it looked just like everywhere else and then tried to get back into the venue. I was stopped by a vicious mountain of a man in police uniform who wouldn't let me pass.

'But I'm with the official Beatles touring party,' I whimpered into his knee-caps. He obviously couldn't believe that anyone so feeble could possbily have anything to do with the tour and replied: 'Sure buddy, and I'm Zsa Zsa Gabor.'

I came back with the old 'Pleased to meet you' response and tried to push my way past, which resulted in him shoving his great slab of a hand into my face and pushing me about twenty yards into the street.

'Your superiors will hear of this, my good man,' I cried, as I slunk away. 'The ambassador is a personal friend of mine and your career is as good as over.' But he wasn't even looking in my direction so I just crept away, feeling persecuted, and sent back another ten seconds of my bathroom chat with Paul.

Some of my reports would be almost complete fabrication. I'd invent stories, just to fill time like 'John fell off the stage today,' 'Paul had a boiled egg for breakfast,' 'Ringo coughed twice'. . .anything to keep the Radio London people happy.

Get Back

Going back to life on board the Pirate ship after the tour was, to say the least, anti-climactic. After weeks of zooming around the Hamburger Heaven that is America in the company of the four most famous people on earth, to suddenly find yourself back on a rusty old tub in the North Sea was a little difficult to get used to. It was still fun though, but the conditions on board were a far cry from the air-conditioned comfort of Americal hotel rooms.

We'd still only get to shower once a week, but this didn't matter a lot because we were just a load of blokes together and cleanliness only really seems to matter when you meet new people or consort with delicious-smelling Frenchwomen. Doesn't it?

Weevils Are Better Than Liverpool

I've already mentioned the appalling quality of the food we were served and you can imagine how delighted we were one day when the discovery was made that there was a crate of Cornflakes stashed in the hold. We brought a packet up to the Mess Hall, treating it as though we'd discovered the Holy Grail, each of us carrying a corner. When we had placed it carefully on the table, spotlit it, like the Mastermind chair, and choreographed a whole Cornflake-packet-opening ceremony around this crock of gold, we noticed that the packet seemed to be moving around a lot. We emptied out the cornflakes to discover that most of the box was filled with a writhing mass of weevils!

But, you overestimate our sensibilities if you think that was going to put us off enjoying our prize. We were very hungry and our mouths had been salivating over the thought of cornflakes since the discovery of the packet so we shook the weevils off, skimmed off the top layer of cereal and had ourselves a real good feast! We put up with hell like that on the boat all the time, and the one consoling thought was that it was better than Liverpool. Weevils are better than Liverpool.

There were some quite pretty bits, though, about being on a boat. Especially first thing in the morning, at about half-past five, before the breakfast show began. I'd take my little cup of tea out on deck and, in the summer, watch the sun come up, dispersing the mists to reveal little fishing boats chugging around with the sunshine glinting off all the watery particles. Our alarm clock was a sailor who'd knock on the door half an hour before it was time to go on. I'd stagger around on deck with my cuppa and then go into the studio while two hunky sailors tried to prise my eyelids apart with a crowbar. When I first got on the air in the mornings I'd take things very slowly at first and wake up gently, along with the listeners. I'd get a book of daily horoscopes and read out one forecast in between each record for the first half hour by which time my mouth had ungummed and my brain was beginning to work in what passes for its normal fashion.

On land or sea, being a disc-jockey is very taxing work. First of all you have to walk into the studio and sit down. If you've any energy left after that, the next step is to remove a record from its sleeve, place it on the turntable, put the needle on the beginning of the grooves and press a button which makes it play for the listening trillions. A pretty gruelling existence, I think you'll agree, and one which requires constant nourishment and high-protein foods. Wholesome nosh was not the speciality of any of our cooks on board Radio London, except, that is, for Pancake John whose experience in the culinary art had been gleaned from his ten years in the Merchant Navy and ten years on a motorbike as a rocker. The brilliantine from his hair would drip, glistening and gleaming, in great dollops all over the pans of grub he slaved over, and funnily enough I used to avoid his cooking and live on a diet of Marmite and chip butties. The best form of dieting in the world is to have Pancake John do your cooking for you.

There's No Business. . .

A radio studio, if it's professionally put together, should be a monument to the art of soundproofing: there are all sorts of fabrics and materials which need to be placed in a highly technicalized position to ensure maximum no-outside-noiseness and perfect acoustics for broadcasting. On board ship, the studio was in the bilges and our soundproofing consisted of a mass of blankets hung over the dank, rusty, slimy walls. That's the wonderful thing about working on t'wireless: you can create a wonderful illusion about where you are. If you listened to the Pirates, it sounded as though we were all swathed in mink and had pop stars coming out of our ears in a haze of pink champagne bubbles. In actual fact we sat in a dingy, blanket-ridden little cell which would make the poorest Scout hut in the land seem like the Café Royal.

One day when the tender ship came alongside to unload its cargo of food, water and dirty magazines, the pilot was a little too enthusiastic and rammed our hull, causing a great enormous crack in one of our water tanks just below the water-line. We had to pump all the water into the other tank on the other side, and that gave us a fifteen-degree list which enabled us to fill up the gash before the high seas came along and committed us all to Davy Jones's Locker. The only problem was that we had no hole-plugging gear on board, so we got a massive baked ham from the tender and shoved that in to dam the crack.

Schmuck Off

I've often got into trouble for using naughty words on the wireless. Sometimes there has been just cause for ticking me off, especially when I've said something wicked just to make an effect. But quite often I truly didn't know the meaning of whatever it was I said. I just latch on to words and use them in any context. The silliest objection I ever had was when 'schmuck' was my Word Of The Week and I'd use it in every possible sentence, even if it made no sense. It's just a nice word, isn't it? Go on, enjoy yourself, say it: 'Schmuck.' There, don't you feel better? It's actually a fairly tame Yiddish word which means wimp or toe-rag. Hardly the most offensive or blasphemous word you can think of, but sure enough, we got complaints from some Chief Rabbi somewhere who didn't think 'schmuck' was the sort of word that should be used in public and so I was forbidden to say it over the airwaves. I was fairly cross about the pettiness of this and, to retaliate, decided to be equally petty: my rebellion manifested itself when I scrawled the word all over the soundproofing blankets which hung in the studio. It must have been very encouraging for whoever took over from me to find the whole studio daubed with toe-raggy slogans!

The Kenny and Cash Show which Dave Cash and I did for a while on Radio London (and later on Capital Radio) was born out of nerves more than out of a conscious editorial policy. I was young, green (often literally) and nervous in those days and things didn't seem quite so frightening if there were two of us to share the speaky bits in between tunes. It became quite a bijou-cultette for a while, which was why Capital decided to resurrect the idea years later when both Dave and I were working together again. I have a vivid memory (and a tape to back it up) of the time at Capital when our then Programme Controller, Aidan Day, was producing the Kenny and Cash Show. He was in the studio with us, browsing through the papers to try and find silly bits for us to read. When you're in a radio studio you can tell when the red light is on if the speakers suddenly cut out. Unless they're turned down very low, which, during a breakfast show, they often are because no-one is up to too much noise first thing in the morning. Aidan wasn't aware that the microphone was on and said: 'Ooh, look, here's a jolly bit,' to which I replied (on the air as well as to him): 'Give it here, then,' and snatched the paper from his hand. The next thing millions of listening Londoners heard was Capital's Head-Of-Everything-That-Is shout: 'Oh fuck off, Everett!' I punched a button to play a record and three seconds later Aidan had turned the colour of beetroot. But, as he was the boss, there was nothing anyone could do about it. The episode came back to haunt him on the day he left Capital because a recording of that incident was included on a sort of 'This Is Your Life' tape which he was presented with to remind him forever of the day he said 'that word' on the radio.

Meanwhile, back in the wacky world of watery wireless, our transmitter was constantly switching itself off. In mid-sentence, and usually just before the punch-line to a joke, the bloody thing would click off and my great lines would be snipped in their prime. The reason was that not a lot of thought had gone into the placing and situation of the transmitter which, like me, is a very delicate instrument and needs to be positioned in exactly the right place if it's going to do its job.

Believe it or not, our little rusty tub became a bit of a tourist attraction. People would sail out on day trips and circle us, throwing requests on deck. It was a bit like feeding-time at the zoo, only instead of buns we got little scrungelets of paper chucked at us.

Things, as you gather, were done in a professional but somewhat slapdash manner. Often I wouldn't get in front of the microphone until seconds before I was due to go on the air which added an extra zing to it all. Once I had to be taken off the air in mid-sentence. It was the day after one of the technicians and I had been experimenting with the effects of. . .cough pills! If you take one it cures your cough, two make you a bit drowsy and three put to you sleep. Fifteen put you into something approaching coma-city and that was the number I'd taken. I remember lying in the bunk, trying to figure out how to work my arms and the rest of my anatomy. The technician was leaning over me asking: 'What's it like, man? Good buzz?' I lay there, incapable of speech or anything, and that was the state I was still in ten hours later when I was due to go on the air and be wonderfully entertaining.

I managed to drag myself down to the studio, slumped into a chair, slammed a record on the turntable and sat listening to it, becoming more and more aware that there was no way I was going to be able to ad-lib my way out of this.

In those days we used to read our own commercials live, so I grabbed a script for an ad, turned on the microphone and said: 'Blifghk reg snop tws pfling the grag. . . .' Suddenly there was a flurry of people rushing into the studio who grabbed me and carried me back to my cabin. I'd love to have a recording of that: it made what Reginald Bosanquet used to sound like seem highly articulate. The moral is: if you've got a cough, leave it to God and steer clear of cough pills. . .well, don't take fifteen of the little beasts, anyway.

I remember getting really quite excited about the fact that there were thousands of people all over the country listening to me, and even more excited when Tony Windsor, one of the senior DJs, said: 'Do you realize that all the stars you admire will probably be listening to you at some point?' I conjured up this image of all the people I'd seen on TV, sitting together in a big huddle around a tranny tuned to Radio London and ME! The first famous person I met (I think) was Rolf Harris! He came on board one day to plug a record and I recall thinking how small he was. I'd only seen him on television which, for some reason, distorts the way people look. My Gran used to think that if she got a TV with a bigger screen, she'd be able to see more of the studio. You can tell that I'm not the only daft member of our family.

Religion's Revenge

I was fired from Radio London (and almost everywhere else) for doing something that I really didn't think was particularly silly. Looking back, though, I suppose it wasn't the most diplomatic and clever thing to do. Diplomacy has never been my strong point, you nurd!

I used to do a three-hour stint on the air, plonked in the middle of which was a pre-recorded tape featuring a religious maniac called Garner Ted Armstrong with 'THE PLAIN TRUTH ABOUT THE WORLD TOMORROW!' Armstrong was an American fanatic who would pay thousands of radio stations all over the world to broadcast his visions of gloom and doom and prophesies of the end of the world if everyone didn't revert to godliness and read his magazine *The Plain Truth*. Radio London was paid about £150 a time to play this half-hour tape and I used to send it up rotten because I was annoyed at this Bible-bashing gonkle suddenly interrupting my wacky programme with his drivelly sentences.

One day Armstrong came over to Britain and heard me on the air taking the unmerciful pee out of his rantings and, more important, out of what he was paying £150 per day to have broadcast. He threatened to take his show off the air unless I was disposed of and, after a hurried conference between the bosses, during which their calculators worked out that £150 multiplied by five was a lot more than they could afford to lose, I was swiftly deposited on the nearest tender and placed firmly on dry land. As I chugged back to shore I listened to Radio London on my little tranny and heard Ed Stewart playing *The Carnival is Over* by The Seekers. A little tear coursed down my cheek and sploshed into the North Sea. It was 1966, before Radio One opened, and the only other avenue open in the fight to keep food in the fridge was Radio Luxembourg who took me on for a while.

In those days Luxembourg had a different programme for each record label which was a good way for the companies to get their records heard but wasn't very fair on the listeners. I was put on the Decca show which, along with all the other programmes of that time, operated on the policy of one decent record every ten minutes and a whole load of other Decca stuff in between which was far from good.

I had to say that every record was great, even though I knew most of it was just garbage Decca were plugging hard in order to try and get it off their hands. In my bones I could feel waves of hate coming from the audience saying: 'How can you say that record's good, Ken? It's a load of junk.' So it wasn't the most rewarding way to make a living.

I didn't do the Luxembourg programmes live. They were pre-recorded and transmitted at a later date, and one day I was listening with a bunch of friends to one of the shows as it was broadcast, a show on which I knew there was a really great joke coming up in between records. 'Listen,' I said to them all when I knew the joke was coming up, 'here comes a really great gag.' Everyone stopped talking and listened to my pre-recorded voice saying: 'Did you hear the one about this nun who was walking through the vegetable patch when suddenly a flock of crows came down and. . . .'

Just then a burst of typical Radio Luxembourg interference scranurgled its way over the airwaves, ruining the punch-line! I was furious at the time, and not terribly upset when I was fired from Luxembourg shortly thereafter – until I found out why. Apparently the Decca people who sponsored my programme, and consequently were my only link with cheques, heard one day that I'd smoked a joint! I think I'd done a Press interview and confessed to smoking pot and the Decca Big Men decided that I wasn't the right sort of image for their product. One joint! They didn't even see me do it or even hear me sound stoned on the air, but out I went. Pot was quite common in those days and I used to smoke it not so much for the buzz it gave me as for the slightly naughty feeling you got just for doing it. It was a bit like farting in church. And the ritual was quite jolly too: all of us huddled in a little circle, rolling joints and passing them round and giggling a lot. It's such tame stuff I can't really see what all the fuss was about.

Naughty Substances

I never had any close shaves with Lily Law as a result of my druggy days. I suppose all that will come when they read this book. I'll probably be raided at 4 o'clock in the morning by a brigade of policemen, hunting for naughty substances. But I've got a great idea: I won't let them in! They'd be disappointed anyway, because I'm not into drugs any more. These days I like to be fully aware of what's going on whereas there was a lot to escape from in those earlier days.

I've always thought that if they legalized pot, the economy would grind to a halt, even more than it has already. Pot tends to slow you up and you don't care so much about what's going on around you, whereas a little alcohol acts as a stimulant and makes you rather brash which is good for getting on with life. If everyone smoked pot all the time, we'd all be leaning up against walls going 'Hey' a lot, which wouldn't get anybody anywhere. Life would be one long siesta. The worst thing of all is cocaine. I did quite a binge on the stuff a while ago and, take my word for it, it's awful. Why do it, then? you ask.

I've no idea really, because it only makes you feel bad. Also, you build up a ridiculous psychological dependence on the stuff. It doesn't make you hallucinate or anything like that, it simply makes you talk very deeply and speedily about anything and everything to anybody and everybody. I used to have very deep conversations with people which, in retrospect, were a lot of crap, but at the time I felt I was getting into people's souls and really finding out what they were all about. It's also absurdly expensive and, like Maltesers, highly more-ish, so that in the course of a heavily cocained evening, it's easy to push a hundred quid's worth up your hooter, most of which ends up on your Kleenex the following morning!

The after-effects are ghastly too. I may have been having a fabulous evening, talking to souls and apparently being deep and meaningful all over the place, but the following day I'd have murdered that same person if they so much as coughed. There's nothing good about it at all: coke is bad for your brain, bad for your nose, bad for your wallet. However, enough about naughty substances (for the moment). On with the story.

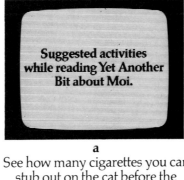

a

See how many cigarettes you can
stub out on the cat before the
phone rings.

b

Wait for the man who's coming
to fix your TV.

c

Invent a new letter of the
alphabet.

d

Re-paint the living room with
Bovril.

TWINKLE, TWINKLE, LITTLE STAR

By this time I'd begun to achieve a certain degree of popularity and notoriety, but I don't recall feeling impressed with myself or thinking: 'Hey, I'm a star.' It was bewildering, more than anything else.

Fame isn't a natural state of affairs, it's not a normal thing to go through, especially if you're from a smoky industrial town and you suddenly find yourself a minor celebrity. I never went through a prima donna phase when I believed myself to be the best thing ever. I still haven't thrown a tantrum about anything to do with work – maybe I'm saving it all up for a blammo-tantrum-eroony!

Nowadays if things don't go quite the way I want them to, I try to be diplomatic and sort things out to my advantage by being nice. There's no point in stamping your feet like the old movie stars used to because everyone around will just dismiss you as difficult to work with. I don't feel secure enough to try and throw my weight around because there are dozens of people around dying to fill the shoes of everyone who's doing quite well and I'm just as dispensable as anyone else. The competition is so fierce that, if I were to stamp around and make life difficult, they'd just look around for someone else. People aren't prepared to waste time soothing egos and rubbing champagne into your eyebrows to calm you down. No matter what the public may think of you, to the people you work with you're just another worker, only you happen to be on the box, or on the radio, and they're behind it, which is just as important.

At the time of writing I'm the flavour of the month as far as the BBC is concerned. By the time you read this I'll probably be working for a bakery again – proof enough that there's no point in deliberately doing things which get up people's noses and get you fired a lot.

Lucy In The Sky With Diamonds

The Sixties were, as we all know, an extraordinary time, especially if you were young. If you weren't, you might as well have been a fish finger, because the decade belonged to youth. Anything and everything seemed possible, especially if you were out of your mind on LSD.

I once took an acid trip with John Lennon on the Weybridge golf course, of all places. John and his sort of court-jester friend Terry Doran had just come out of a club called the Speakeasy in London. I was nattering to them on the pavement when he was besieged by a flurry of fans, causing him to retreat hastily into his car and scoot away. The two of them were obviously on something because John was talking

This chapter illustrated by Robin Harris.

completely incomprehensible drivel and Tony was not only understanding what was being said, but replying in the same off-the-planet vein.

I lay in the back of the car, listening to all this going on, thinking: 'If I lie low and don't say anything, they'll forget I'm here and drive all the way to John's house in Weybridge. I'll be able to see the inside of the house and maybe stay a while.'

The car cruised past Lower Sloane Street, where my hovel was situated, and carried on all the way to Weybridge. The other two were talking about all sorts of things which made sense only to them. As we crunched up the drive of John's house, I poked my nose up from the back and said: 'Oh, I say, you've gone past my flat. What a pity.'

John said something like: 'Life is a bacon-butty,' which I took to mean 'Come on in, Ken,' so I did. Into this Aladdin's Cave of a house with acres of grounds and a brace of swimming pools in the bathroom. I'd never seen anything like it and followed the two of them into the kitchen where Terry produced and cooked up a can of Heinz Tomato Soup. I thought: 'Wow, John Lennon eats Heinz Tomato Soup – how ordinary. I thought he'd have had turtles' eggs flown in from Bangkok and caviar freshly rolled on the hips of Filipino virgins.'

There was no way I could communicate with either of them in their current state, but I slept the night there and the next day John asked if I wanted some LSD. I thought: 'Yes, John. Anything you say John. Tell me to turn into a pickled gherkin and I'll do it.' So we popped this stuff into our mouths and ten minutes later I was wondering what exactly I was and where I was and why I was and was I why and who where was. . . . John said: 'Let's go for a walk,' and I remember it was raining very gently – the sort of upper-class, fine rain you could only find in posh places like Weybridge. It was very quiet and the air smelled of pine trees as we wafted along, dressed in psychedelic cloaks. We walked on to the golf course and suddenly a helicopter landed. I've no idea why and it's just the sort of surreal thing you'd imagine when you are tripping, but it definitely happened. Or was it a bird?

I had no idea what was happening to my brain as the chemical worked its way around my untutored particles. It's impossible to describe a trip, but it's a bit like *2001* on toast and for a while you believe you've discovered the secret of life and the meaning of the universe. A few hours later, when the chemical has used up ten billion of your brain cells, it deposits you back at square one and leaves you simply bewildered. You can't remember anything about the secrets you've supposedly been taught while tripping because the experience is so far removed from anything your real brain can handle. It would be rather like someone from the twentieth century wandering up to a caveman and saying: 'Hi, there are great things coming, you know, like colour television and the microwave oven and the wheel – the wheel's a round thing with spokes and it will help you get to places and make machines function.' The modern-day man would then disappear leaving the caveman scratching his head: 'Wheel? I remember it was a great idea, but I can't remember exactly what it was or how it worked.'

LSD is extraordinary and interesting stuff, but not to be recommended. It was all just part of the times, and after the trip with John I experimented many times with the stuff over the years until I came to the conclusion that real life was actually just as jolly and much more intriguing than any hallucination.

A couple of months after my psychedelic round of golf with John I was in the Abbey Road recording studios where The Beatles were recording *I am a Walrus*. George Martin, their producer, was working with John on the vocal track and he said: 'Look, you've been singing now for about seven hours, you're beginning to sound hoarse, why don't we do it tomorrow?' John wanted to get it done that day

and that's why he sounds so raucous on that track.

When he got to the line about getting a tan from standing in the English rain, he stopped and said to me: 'Reminds me of that day on the Weybridge golf course, hey Ken,' to which I replied: 'What?'

'You remember,' he said, 'the Weybridge golf course. . .the rain. . .get a tan from standing. . .oh, forget it.'

I'm sure he always thought I was a complete lemon. . .or was it a bird?

All Good Things. . .

The jolly days aboard the Pirate ships couldn't last forever. Everyone was having too much fun and I remember feeling very clever, about six months before the whole thing folded, when I thought to myself that the government's attack on Pirate radio was gathering momentum and now was the time to plan ahead and get on with The Future. The government had realized that, as the law stood, Radio London and all the others were legal in as much as they were situated three miles from land and were therefore in Anybody's Space and unputintojailable. We were still annoying to them though, and their great Bureaucrat Brain cranked into gear and came up with the ideal solution: change the law.

Clever old Ken decided that the BBC would have to produce something to keep the pop-tune loving public from rioting in the streets when the Pirates were closed down. I decided to make friends within the Beeb so that when its answer to the Pirates arrived I'd be Mister Big by the time all the other DJs came looking for work. Clever, huh? So I infiltrated myself into the ranks of the BBC workers and spent a lot of time in the canteen, having arranged with the switchboard to be paged regularly so that my name would begin to register in the minds of those who controlled the whole outfit.

But my clever idea was overshadowed by my lack of tact which reared its ugly head one day when I was invited by Derek Chinnery (who'd luckily forgotten the mess I'd made of my audition years earlier) to come and watch the Pete Murray Show being broadcast. I sat in the control room fascinated by the mammoth production which was going on around me: Pete Murray sat in the studio in front of the microphone, surrounded by bits of paper and scripts (which were taboo on the Pirates). On the other side of the glass sat a technician working the gramophones, another technician working the tape machines, *another* one operating the volume controls, somebody telling those three what to do and Derek Chinnery overseeing the whole thing. I couldn't understand the point of all these people, especially considering that what went out on the air was no better than what the Pirates did, with no production staff and no scripts. With all the folly of youth at my disposal, I walked up to Derek, who'd been producing programmes since 1066, and said: 'Now listen here, you're doing this all wrong.'

It was little things like that which didn't exactly endear me to the Beeb's Big Wheels and thwarted my master plan. Meanwhile, all the polite Pirate DJs like Tony Blackburn and Ed Stewart instantly got jobs the moment Radio One opened, leaving me to twiddle my thumbs in Lower Sloane Street. I did get a programme on Radio One in the early days called *Midday Spin* which was a record-review programme designed to get around the fact that every time a radio station plays a record it has to pay a royalty to the people who made and published it. Think of how many records are played per day and you'll see how that can soon mount up to a lot of money. One way round it in those days was to introduce each disc with a half-hearted review like: 'Here's one that's not too bad, on the Decca label, F13412.' I did an hour of this every Tuesday lunchtime for a while, seething every morning as I'd hear Tony Blackburn doing his three-hour, daily breakfast show. Aaargh!

―――――――――――――――――― **Life Is An Orange** ――――――――――――――――――

My first-ever encounter with my wife, Lady Lee, was in 1966 at a house which was owned by Brian Epstein, The Beatles' manager.

These days, when you go to a party, the host will ask what you'd like to drink. In the Sixties you were asked what you'd like to blow your mind – especially if you were at a groovy, fab gear pop party! Lee was sitting chatting to Ringo Starr, Klaus Voorman, John Lennon and George Harrison. I, apparently, was just sprawled out on the floor. At least, my body was on the floor, my brain was floating on another planet in an LSD-induced trance. Lee says that she was first attracted, well, perhaps attracted is the wrong word, Lee first *noticed* me because I was the whitest creature she'd ever set eyes upon. George, I'm told (I remember very little of this period), came over to me and tried to explain The Secret Of Life with helpful, easily understandable lines like: 'It's all around you, Ken. . .you know, like. . . life is an orange – it's everywhere.' Is it any wonder I was confused?

At that stage, George was heavily into religion, bells and beads, and whenever he moved he sounded like Tinkerbell. After trying to explain what It Was All About, he jangled his way around the room for a while and came back to sit next to me. Lee rolled a joint and passed it around; she had a knack of always keeping track of who was holding the joint. It had reached George who was holding it, not smoking it, but just talking while the pot burned away. Lee got fed up with watching her precious drugs being wasted and she said: 'George, you're hogging the joint.' He turned on Lee and told her to piss off, which she didn't think was very spiritual for someone who was preaching about how wonderful God was, so she said: 'That's very un-Christly of you, George.' He stood up, fixed her with a custard-curdling glare and jangled away into the distance. John Lennon, who was off his head on something or other, burst out laughing and fell off his chair. Ringo patted Lee on the back and said: 'Well done, Lee.' I think they were a bit fed up with George at that point because he was ramming religion down everybody's throat at every opportunity.

As I said, I'm not too clear about that period. My brain was in a state of constant scrambled-eggness, but that, according to Lady Lee, is where she first set eyes on the skinny white rib-on-a-stick that would later whisk her into transports of delight.

Some while later, I went to see a friend called Don Paul who was the middle Count in a group called the Viscounts (remember *Who Put the Bomp*?). He lived in a flat in Fulham which was filled with a strange mixture of arty weirdos like a sex-change frock designer and a man who tattooed goldfish, and one day we were all lying around this flat smoking pot when in walked Billy Fury with his almost-wife, who was Lee! They invited us all to their mansion in Sussex which Billy had bought with the money he'd made from *Halfway to Paradise* and all his other hits.

Most people about to take a car journey to Sussex might take the precaution of going to the loo and packing a sandwich. We threw LSD down ourselves and squanged into Lee's little car all believing we were pineapples.

Billy and Lee were nearing the end of their time together and she and I got quite chummy over the next few months. I'd pack up every weekend and go down to their house where we'd all sit in the sunshine, taking LSD by the bucketful.

I remember one weekend at the house when a rather eccentric BBC producer came along for fun, bringing with him a tin filled with LSD and purple hearts and anything else which was available in those days. We were relying on this tin to see us through two days of lunacy and we were all having a silly time when suddenly the sound of a police-car siren shattered the still of the country air.

The man with the tin suddenly had this image of screaming newspaper headlines: 'BBC PRODUCER IN DRUG RAID AT POP STAR'S ORGY PARTY SHOCK HORROR PROBE', so he grabbed the contents of the magic box and threw them as hard as possible into the forest which backed onto Billy's garden. Dozens of little pills hurtled into the air and came to rest among the bracken and long grass which lay all around the house.

The siren came closer and closer and CLOSER and then. . .receded into the distance leaving all of us in a homicidal rage at the poor, frightened man from the BBC who'd scattered the precious capsules as far as the eye couldn't see.

We grabbed him by the scruff of the neck and forced him to show us exactly where he'd been standing and in precisely which direction he chucked the drugs and then all of us spent hours scrabbling around on our hands and knees in a desperate search for the naughty but nice things which were buried in the ferns. Eventually we found one little pill which we portioned up into tiny morsels and greedily shared amongst us. Silly days. I wouldn't like to go back, but I wouldn't have missed it either.

Clunk Click – Every Trip

There now follows a non-government warning about LSD based on personal experience. I think this episode happened on my first visit to Billy Fury's house, when we were all tripping away merrily. I was staring at my hand and noticed, as if for the first time, all the veins that were sticking up, the way veins are supposed to.

My electrified brain started behaving in the most peculiar way and I became very worried about the fact that inside my body was a stomach, kidneys, liver, bones, blood, lungs. . .all sorts of flobbelly bits, oozing all over the place. I suddenly became convinced that the only decent thing to do was end it all.

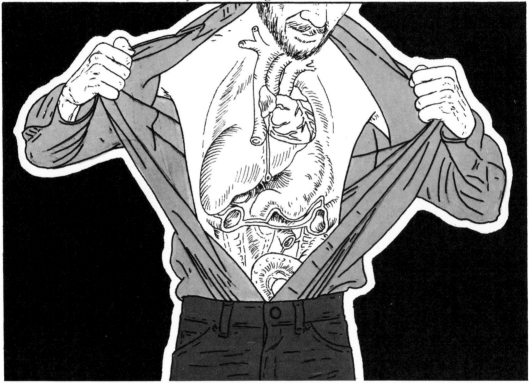

'Hey,' I shouted to the rest of the bunch of pineapples, 'we're all walking masses of blood and guts! It's horrible. . .we've all got to commit suicide.'

It sounds daft now, but at the time, with my brain in its pickled state, it seemed as though I'd made the most logical and brilliant discovery of all time.

'I'm going to do it now,' I said, filled with the righteousness of my conviction, and began to hunt around for a sharp implement.

Lee said: 'Look, if you're going to kill yourself, could you do it outside? We've just bought this new carpet, you see. . . .' I was angry at not being taken seriously, but then she began to talk to me. 'What do you want to die for? There are so many lovely things about.'

'Like what?' I harrumphed.

'Like that pine tree over there.'

'What's so great about pine trees?'

'Well, they make the air smell nice and they're pretty to look at.'

We talked on for a while in this rather facile but quite pleasant vein and gradually she talked me out of it. I'm not sure that I'd actually have committed suicide but she definitely started me thinking about the right way to look at things and to appreciate the value of all the good bits in the world. She taught me to look for the good in everything and not worry about the bad: accentuate the positive, eliminate the negative and place for half an hour in a pre-heated oven.

Cherchez La Femme (whatever that means)

Lee obviously had decided to take pity on this little, white, skinny runt and she talked to me for hours. For my part, I wasn't very good at social niceties and I'd do selfish, silly things which would make her mad and which once caused her to ban me from the house. She had a collection of fans of which she was very proud. Billy would buy her dozens of beautiful, ornate, exotic fans from auctions and private collections and she built up a whole mass of pretty, feathery, jewelled fans. At one party at her house I was (apparently) sitting on the floor, fanning myself with a very rare and expensive fan which had been salvaged from the Russian Czar's family and which was worth a small fortune. Lee told me to be careful with it. 'Why?' I said, 'it's only a fan.' I promptly broke it and although she was very upset by my lack of respect for other people's treasures, she let the incident pass.

An hour later I was discovered fiddling with a set of beautiful, hand-painted beads, again worth a small fortune and of great sentimental value to Lee. 'Now look here,' she said, 'you've already broken my fan, for God's sake be careful with those.' 'Why?' I said, 'they're only beads.' The next moment, the string snapped and hundreds of delicate bijou-beadettes went hurtling onto the floor and were trampled underfoot and broken. Lee was livid and banned me from the house. 'I don't want you in my home,' she said, 'I don't want you near my home. I don't want you to ring me. I don't ever want to see you again. Out!' So out I went, wondering what all the fuss was about.

A couple of weeks later, I decided that I rather missed Lee and her fun parties so I sent a letter promising not to break anything, promising to respect other people's possessions, promising to try and learn some manners. I covered the letter with little drawings of broken hearts and tears; I was allowed back into the scene.

Shortly afterwards, Lee and Billy split up and, obviously, after eight years together, she was pretty upset and cried a lot. I wasn't too sure what one was supposed to do with a crying woman, but I did my best and helped her get back on her feet and pick up again in London. She decided to fling herself around at parties and have a whale of a time and there were quite a lot of chaps interested in her but, according to her, no-one else stood a chance. It wasn't because I swept her off her feet onto a white charger. It was that I simply made a nuisance of myself and developed a knack of turning up at the wrong moment when she was just getting interested in another feller.

I once phoned her at a highly inopportune moment to say that I was just about to go to the BBC to do a programme on Radio One and, if she listened, I'd play her some records. She said that she didn't have a radio. Determined not to be thwarted, I popped into her flat on my way to the studio and gave her a radio. . .thereby putting paid to one rival!

Lee goes all gooey when she remembers our 'courting' days. I bought her a huge paper flower once, from Casa Pupo. It was the same height as her and we became very attached to the flower and used to take it into the country at weekends for walks and sunshine. Although I'm a romantic at heart and like to play all the games of courtship, I didn't in those days have the first clue about how to approach a woman and entice her into my bed. I was yer actual innocent virgin! I was so uncertain about how to go about getting things started that, when Lee and I took a holiday together on the Continent while she was trying to sort herself out over Billy, I spent the whole fortnight in fear of the night-time. We were driving all over the place and my foot was fixed firmly to the accelerator most of the time. I dreaded nights when we'd have to find a hotel and we'd often go to three or four hotels until I could find one which had two vacant rooms. She told me later that the last thing on her mind at that point was beginning another affair. She just needed to relax and not to have to think about men, but I was so unsure of myself that I completely over-reacted and spent the whole holiday trying to think of ruses so we wouldn't have to sleep together.

One night we were tripping in my little flat in Lower Sloane Street, and the LSD was making all the good bits about life great and all the bad bits even worse. I looked around the room and the only nice thing I could see was Lee. The acid made her look even prettier and it was as though there was an aura surrounding her body. Without thinking I just said: 'Good heavens, you're the prettiest thing in this room,' and she went terribly coy and demure.

I hadn't a clue how to proceed from that point, but somehow, fumblingly, we managed to make some sort of love. The next day we did it again, a little less fumblingly, and things proceeded from there.

Lee and I got closer and closer as time went on, and at a party at Don Paul's one night when were all being after dinner mints (yes, tripping again), I got the horrors. Every now and again when you're taking LSD, things go wrong. A word here, a movement there, the slightest thing can set you off into an explosion of horrendous fright and terror. I sat quivering in a corner and looked around the room. My eyes alighted on Lee and I thought: 'She's the only person I want to be with while I'm going through this awful experience. So it seems only natural that we should be together for life.'

When my brain had de-scrambled itself, Lee and I went for a walk to get some fresh air and we stopped under a magnolia tree. I thought: 'This looks like a good place to propose,' but I couldn't bring myself actually to say the words.

We returned to the house and I asked Don if he would ask Lee on my behalf to be my wife. The swine said no, so I took her back to the tree and said, in my best Cary Grant voice:

'I suppose we'd better get married, then.'

'I suppose so,' said Lee, and that was that. Not exactly a Doris Day-type proposal, but then again, I'm not exactly Doris Day.

──────────────── **Dearly Beloved. . .(Hic)** ────────────────

When Lee was trying to sort out what she'd wear to get married in we spent hours wandering around shops trying to find the perfect bit of lace. We saw yards and yards of stuff, but nothing was quite right. We were just about to give up and dress her in a set of bin-liners when one day we passed some nice tablecloths on our way out of the shop. 'That's nice,' said Lee. 'Yes, madam,' said the assistant, 'and it seats twelve people.' We bought it and chopped it about so that Lee could get married in a twelve-seater tablecloth which cost £3. 10s. . . ah, remember good old shillings.

Soon enough we were at the registry office, surrounded by a collection of Sixties weirdos. Tony King, who's now in America and for a while was one of Elton John's entourage, organized the whole event. He hired a double-decker bus to ferry all the guests, and we arrived in a horse-drawn carriage, driven by a man with a top hat and a whip: Lee in her tablecloth, me in a mega-natty Edwardian suit with a pink cravat. It was very embarrassing really. You attract a lot of attention, crawling slowly along Kensington High Street in a horse-drawn carriage. You should try it. The Press were there in full force and it must have been a bad day for real news, because we got a lot of coverage, including a complaint in the local paper from a lady who said that we were taking the mickey out of marriage with such a vulgar display of merriment and turning the whole affair into a party – which is what I always thought weddings were about in the first place. We'd even decided to have the reception before the ceremony, which is a great idea, because it takes the seriousness out of the whole affair.

My Mother nearly fainted during the ceremony because she wasn't aware that I'd legally changed my name to Kenny Everett and when the man said: 'Do you, Kenny Everett, take this woman, etc,' a squeaky Liverpool voice at the back of the room screeched: 'Ooh, it's not legal!' A couple of gay friends we knew stood behind us during the ceremony and got married at the same time. Sweet, huh?

The sex-change person who was part of our social scene in those days made a great punch for the party afterwards. He/she had also spiked the drink with all sorts of pills which made everyone rabbit on into the small hours of our wedding night. Except me, because I was the only one who didn't have any of the laced punch, so I left them all yattering away and toddled off to bed by myself.

——————————————— **My Animals And Other Family** ———————————————

Our first marital home was in Holland Road, Holland Park, and what a dump it was. Very cheap though, because all the local cats had made it into their latrine and it stank to high heaven. Gallons of Sanilav later, we turned the flat into quite a blissful place which Lee filled with animals. We both decided very early on that children were nasty, noisy, rude sticky things to be steered clear of at all costs. Instead we accumulated a menagerie which included a chihuahua, an African Grey parrot called Smokey, a macaw, two cats, a Great Dane and a monkey which used to claw things to pieces and rush around the flat playing merry hell. We bought a big cage which the monkey was none too keen on and, to show its displeasure, it used to shit in its hands and chuck it through the bars.

The zoo's next addition was a rabbit which didn't last long because the Great Dane decided to cuddle it one day with its huge paws and it broke the rabbit's back. We arrived home to see the dog pushing a little furry bundle around the room as if to say: 'Come on, why have you stopped playing?'

All these animals in a two-foot-square basement in Holland Park: no wonder the neighbours never came round to borrow cups of sugar.

y first jaunt into the land of television was a programme for Granada TV called *Nice Time* which I did with Jonathan Routh and Germaine Greer. I almost didn't get the programme, because when the producer called my agent to ask me to do the series, she said: 'Oh, don't have Everett, he's unreliable, have Tony Blackburn instead.' Funnily enough, I left that agent soon after and moved to the lady who looks after me now, Jo Gurnett, who's a sweetiepie. And who also looks after Terry Wogan.

Nice Time was a collection of silly sketches and dopey gags. Nowadays they have Portaprompt, or Autocue which is a sort of rolling scroll on which your lines are written. In those days there was no such luxury and I'd have to go through the nightmare of learning lines, which terrified me; I'm still no good at it.

I had to go up to Manchester once a week to do the programme. In those days I had a little Fiat 850 which is like an electric kettle on wheels, and no good at all for long journeys.

Appearing on TV brings with it fame, money, sacks of mail. . .and the horror of being recognizable to thousands of people. Being famous on the radio is lovely because you get nice little perks like better tables in restaurants without the invasion of privacy, whereas having a face well-known because of television is a terrible thing to live with. There's nothing worse, when you're feeling low and you nip to Safeway for a tin of peas, than being surrounded instantly by dozens of voices going: 'Oooh, look, it's 'im. 'Allo, Ken, do us a sketch, be funny.' Someone at a party went up to Noel Coward (who is responsible for the title of this chapter) and said: 'Say something funny,' to which Coward replied: 'Kangaroo,' and turned away. That's how I feel when people say things like that. Sometimes, of course, it's quite nice. If a lady potters up and says something like: 'Ee, you were a daft bugger on the telly last night,' that's lovely, but I'm not good at doing cabarets on the spot, especially when I'm feeling a bit morose. It's a terrible trap, because if you're not charming and pleasant to everyone in the street, all the time, they'll accuse you of being big-time and a prima donna. But think how *you'd* feel if every time you were in a restaurant, or a shop, or a cinema, there was a chorus of 'Say something funny'. You might think it would be flattering and a great boost to your ego, which to some people it must be, but not day in day out, year in year out.

I was in a restaurant not long ago with my Radio Two producer, just having a quiet lunch, talking about the programme. Suddenly this drunken, leery face

lurched under my nose from the next table and said: 'Your show's a load of fucking crap.' Fair enough, he may feel that way, but I think what probably prompts people to do things like that is so they can go home to their wives and say: 'I told Kenny Everett where to get off today, aren't I great?'

I don't mind people who ask for autographs and then happily toddle off. But it's the people who assume that, because you're on TV, you're convinced that you're better than they are, so they go to great lengths to show you you're not.

The only places I can go and not get bothered are fairly ritzy (and very expensive!) restaurants where everyone else is more famous than me and nobody cares who's at the next table. That's why places become trendy and populated by 'stars' but, of course, what happens is that people start to go there because they want to sit next to Michael Caine or whoever. As soon as that happens, the people with well-known faces find some other place to hide and tuck into their spaghetti, and the old restaurant is filled with disappointed star-spotters.

The real answer to the hundreds of people every week who say: 'You're Kenny Everett, aren't you?' is: 'Yes, I am,' but that sounds a bit severe, so I launch into a little routine to send them away happy (which gets very wearing when it happens twenty times a day). I don't mean to sound snotty, but the nicest thing you can do if you feel moved to approach a 'celebrity' when he or she is having a quiet nosh, or buying kitchen towels, is just say 'Hello' and move on. They'll really appreciate you for being thoughtful.

Watching yourself on the box can be severely embarrassing if you've done something that you know in your heart of hearts is not quite up to standard. It's also lovely, of course, if you're proud of your work.

Years ago I did a TV series for London Weekend Television, just after colour television had been introduced, and I thought: 'Great, everyone will be looking at the colour, not at me!' The producers stuck me in front of a camera and, assuming that I could ad-lib on TV the same as I do on radio, I was supposed to be wacky and zany for half an hour with no script! I died a thousand deaths a second. To save the day they brought on a monkey, hoping that the beast and I could do wonderfully funny routines with a bunch of bean bags. The monkey stank and just sat there, picking fleas out of its armpits. Great TV!

A-U-N-T-I-E Turns Ugly

After the Pirates had closed down and most of the DJs had wound up on Radio One, the sense of Pirate unity dissolved somewhat. Instead of all the guys on Radio London being one unit, and at the same time allies of the guys from Caroline, all fighting the grey monolith that was the BBC, the only thing left to fight was each other. Egos began to blow up a bit and, inevitably, this led to conflict and competition. A lot of the chumminess just disappeared, and it hasn't really come back. Even now, most DJs are more concerned with their own careers than with whichever station they're working for. The sense of being part of an entity has gone and it's easy to see why. There's not a lot to feel cuddly about when you walk through the vast doors of the BBC in Portland Place.

I was eventually given a Saturday morning show which replaced Brian

Matthew's. It was produced by Angela Bond, a lady with boobs from here to John O'Groats. She was lovely, and used to mother me through the programmes, but she lived in constant fear of my overstepping the bounds of what was considered decent. The Beeb's idea of that differed greatly from my own and I was always getting into trouble for saying almost-rude words and generally misbehaving.

As everyone knows, I was fired from the BBC for being a naughty boy. What used to annoy the Heads-Of-Everything-That-Is most was the way I'd talk to the Press about my employers. Journalists would ask me what life was like at the Beeb compared to the carefree old days on the Pirates. The people who ran Radio One were quite proud of what they thought of as a jolly, exciting venture and the last thing they wanted to see was undiplomatic old me quoted in the papers as saying that the place was filled with mahogany people with mahogany minds, all falling asleep and with about as much get-up-and-go as a tortoise on valium.

The papers loved it, of course. 'DULL DULL DULL, SAYS CUDDLY KEN', and 'THE BBC IS NO PLACE TO BE', but after about four or five of these articles had appeared I was summoned to the office of Douglas Muggeridge, Chief-of-Heads-of-Everything-That-is-And-Ever-Will-Be, who told me that I had to stop slagging off the Beeb and made me sign a piece of paper to the effect that if I did it again, I'd be dispensed with.

The next newspaper person who asked me what I thought of the Beeb was told: 'I'm terribly sorry, but I've signed a piece of paper which says that I won't speak to the Press about how awful Radio One is.' Next day: 'BEEB GAGS CUDDLY KEN', which naturally annoyed the hierarchy even more.

On the next programme I did, I made some crack about the wife of the then Minister of Transport bribing the driving examiner so she'd pass her test. It was just the excuse the BBC needed. 'Got him,' they cried with glee and I received a phone-call informing me that my services were no longer required. I wasn't too dismayed because I'd just signed with London Weekend Television, so there was a glimmer of cheques still on the horizon and I didn't have a mortgage or any major commitments, apart from a monkey, Great Dane, parrot, macaw, rabbit. . . .

I phoned Jonathan King and told him I'd been fired. JK called his publicist, David Block, to try and organize some newspaper coverage, and within a couple of hours my little flat was seething with reporters who swigged down a crateload of champagne I'd dashed out to buy especially for the occasion. If you ever want to get

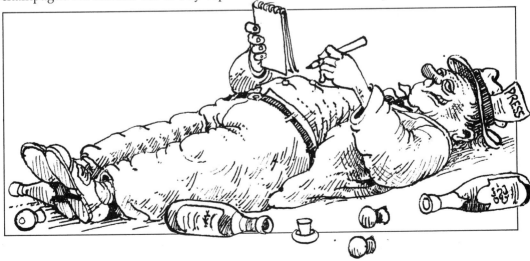

the newspapers to take your side, feed them champagne. The photographers told me to look sad, so I put on my Clement Freud face and Lee patted me on the head and we said how could the mighty monolith that is the BBC wreak this terrible revenge on little two-foot-six Cuddly Ken?

The following day there were yards and yards of words and pictures all over the papers, and all on my side. The reports were wonderfully sympathetic to my case and I suspect the BBC were rather upset by the way the story was angled. If I hadn't been involved and had just read the newspaper stories, I would have thought: 'How can they do that to this poor young, miniature innocent DJ?' It made the Beeb out to be villains which, of course, doesn't matter all that much because they can just lock themselves away in their labyrinth and wait for all the fuss to die down, which they did.

There followed a bijou-outcry-ette from the public. Car stickers appeared saying 'Bring Back Everett', and Katie Boyle wrote a protesting letter to the papers saying that she'd never in all her born days heard of anything so unjust. Which was going a bit over the top: it wasn't as if the BBC had invaded Poland, after all. Still, it was all quite flattering, and fun.

Lee has kept scrapbooks of Press cuttings from over the years and the biggest section in those books is about my sacking from the BBC. My favourite article to do with the whole silly affair was this one which appeared in a posh paper and made the tiny event seem like a major international incident:
'Lord Hill, chairman of the BBC governors, has denied that the dismissal of the disc-jockey, Kenny Everett, involved a change of policy. He was replying to a letter in

which Mr Gerald Kaufman, MP for Ardwick, Manchester, said personal attacks of extraordinary virulence – though often couched in humorous terms – had been made on members of the Labour goverment without such immediate and stringent action. Lord Hill said that Mr Everett's remark about Mrs John Peyton, the Transport Minister's wife, passing the advanced driving test would have been equally offensive if made about any member of the public. Apologies similar to that sent to Mrs Peyton had gone to the driving examiner concerned and to the Institute of Advanced Motorists. In a letter to Mr Kaufman, released yesterday, Lord Hill said: "We have made it clear that this remark was not the main reason for the action taken. Mr Everett has, on a number of occasions, made remarks about broadcasting matters of a kind likely to be damaging to the BBC and its relations with outside bodies." Kenny Everett yesterday let fly at the BBC's "pinstripe princes" who, he said, made the decisions but could not understand pop music.'

Isn't that fab?! I love the thought of Lords and MPs bickering and arguing over tiny me.

Poor Noel Edmonds was the one who replaced me on Radio One after I was given the elbow. These days he's a multi-billionaire with helicopters, mansions and an endless supply of Cup-A-Soup, but when he occupied the hot seat following my ignominious departure from the Beeb he was 21 and no-one had ever heard of him. In an interview with Noel published just before he took over from me, he said: 'I doubt whether many people will take to me because I'm the one who's taken over from the one everybody liked.' (What a complicated sentence for someone who was planning to make his living being a disc-jockey.)

Later on in my (for want of a better word) career, the BBC took me back for a bit, but they were highly sneaky about it. Instead of just sticking me back on Radio One, they decided to break me in gently and make me prove that I was going to be a good boy by giving me shows to do on BBC local radio stations like Brighton, Solent and Nottingham which have a collective audience of about seven people and two sheep. That way, if I misbehaved no-one would notice and I would be consigned back to the dole queue without any egg appearing on Broadcasting House itself. The Radio Bristol programme was a real mindbender of a show, as you can imagine from this quote by its producer, Mike Fitzgerald: 'The idea is that anyone in the West with a claim to fame may appear. We'll be meeting the world bowls champion, the captain of Britain's sea-angling team, a Gloucestershire man who claims he's spoken to men from Outer Space who are frequenting Cirencester Common and numerous others who reckon they're the champs in some way or other.' Well, with a line-up of guests like that I can't imagine how I managed to drag myself away from Radio Bristol, can you, darling reader?

THE OUT OF TOWNERS

n about nineteen-sixty-something-or-other, Lee and I decided to 'get away from it all' and go and live in the country. We tootled around Sussex and found a beautiful old farmhouse in Cowfold in which every room leaned in a different direction. On our first night there we sat around a big roaring fire, which promptly set fire to the wooden bits that covered the whole house and we spent our first night in the country shovelling buckets of water onto our own towering inferno.

While we were in Cowfold I bought a bunch of wonderful technical equipment which I had installed at the house so that I could do my own programmes at home and be on the radio without ever leaving my fourteen acres of loveliness. It was from this little secluded unit that I made my comeback on Radio One. They eventually relented and asked me to do one show per week, but they insisted that it should be on tape so that nothing untoward could go out on the air. That was fine by me because it saved a journey into London. The only thing wrong with the arrangement was that I couldn't do time-checks on the programme which, if you listen carefully, take up a lot of speech-space on most DJ shows. If you're clever and lazy, you can even build up to a time-check with jingles and fanfares, thereby saving your brain buds a lot of energy in thinking up something zany to say. 'It's almost time-check time!' The other problem was that the machine which times how long a piece of tape lasts didn't work in my studio at home, so instead of the required half-hour they'd get twenty-six-and-a-half minutes and have to fill the remaining bit with jingles and promotions for up-coming programmes.

But the nervous old Beeb still chopped out the strangest bits from my tapes. There was one instance when I played a record by The Four Tops called *Ain't No Woman Like The One I Love*, and I said: 'That's The Four Tops with *Ain't No Woman Like My One-eyed Love*,' and they chopped it out. I suppose they thought they'd get a lot of letters from complaining one-eyed women, but it seemed daft enough to me not to be offensive to anyone.

Lee and I stayed in Sussex for a while before deciding to move even further away from the throbbing metropolis: to Wales. I think they must have had a big sale of pink paint one day years ago in Wales, because everything we saw was pink. Eventually we discovered a place on a mountain top in Llandovery which wasn't pink and looked quite nice because the woman we bought it from had cleaned it up before our arrival, including the farm area that came with it; she'd mowed the curtains and polished the cows and it really looked rather pleasant.

It was very picturesque and had masses of land with it which stretched from

This chapter illustrated by Dan Pearce.

Dan Pearce '82

the mountain tops where the house was right down to a stream at the bottom. What we didn't know before we bought it was that it's bloody cold on mountain tops and that Wales is the rainiest place in the world. The only time it doesn't rain in Wales is when you're leaving to go to do a job in London.

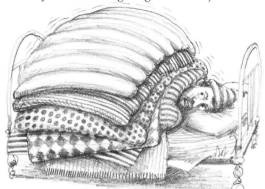

On our first night there the icicles had icicles. It was the coldest night for centuries and there were cows skating around everywhere you looked. All the sheep had congregated at the bottom of the mountain in a vast woolly huddle, trying to keep warm. I remember arriving there and not thinking, as you're supposed to when you move into a new house: 'Won't it be fab,' but: 'Oops, big boob, Ken.' The nearest point of comfort was London which is a long way to go to warm your toes, so we just looked forlornly around the frozen wastes of our new kingdom and decided to go to bed. The Great Dane, Bosie, almost died of cold that night. We put the electric blanket on top of him to try and keep him warm. . .but we forgot to plug it in, so we woke up the following morning to find this blue Great Dane shivering at the bottom of the bed. Quite often, I'd wake up in the middle of the night, purple with cold, to discover that Lee had gone in search of extra warmth to some other part of the house. I once found her sleeping in the bath because we had one of those strip-heaters in the bathroom and she was trying it out for warmth.

The first morning, we got up, filled ourselves with stoic resolve and decided that the only thing to do was make the place a little paradise; we'd stick it until we could stand it no longer. We hired some builders who installed the studio equipment in our new cowshed. They managed to do that all right, but when it came to laying carpet – forgetitsville! It looked like the Atlantic Ocean in the middle of a Force Nine gale. There were great runkles gathered at every corner, like a bloodhound's face. We spent a fortune on the house but it never really felt like home. The best bit was the studio which was insulated and sound-proofed and double-glazed. But, of course, when we came to sell it, there aren't too many Welsh farmers who require a mountain-top radio studio in a cowshed. With the house came a herd of cows which we'd milk first thing in the morning. Have you ever milked a cow? No? Well, keep it that way. I had to cover my hands with Udsal which makes the cow's teats easier to get hold of. Then

I'd grab these great, flobbelly dangly bits and squeeze away for hours, all for about two millilitres of milk. After ten minutes of squeezing, my little townie's hands would get tired so I'd have to take a break in order to get some life back into them and then come back and finish the job. You had to make sure every cow was properly milked, otherwise she'd explode!

The other delightful aspect of my time as a dairyman was when, having milked bucketsful of creamy gunge from the bowels of the beasts, they performed nature's most natural function which splunged all over the milking area and, more often than not, right into the pails of milk, making a rather unsavoury chocolate milk-shake. The only options then were: either pour the liquid down the grid, or back into the front end of the cow.

The cows were kept happy by the presence of a large Hereford bull who looked as though he had a bunch of melons dangling from his stomach and frightened old ladies throughout the neighbourhood. Our prowess as farmers left a lot to be desired and the poor bull would get dirtier and dirtier as he was left for longer and longer periods without anyone 'clearing up': pulling his chain, so to speak. (It's not easy being delicate about such matters you know.) As we were terrified of him, we couldn't just go up and say: 'Excuse me, can we do you now?' so the situation got worse and worse until he just got stuck in the gunk.

The cows carried on manufacturing milk day after day but, as we weren't a commercial outfit, it was far too much for us to make good use of, so we bought a make-your-own-cream machine from a looney lady who lived on top of the next hill. We then enjoyed two days of cream on everything: cornflakes, scones, steaks, fish, everything was doused in thick, delicious cream. Of course, after a couple of days,

the novelty wore off and instead of gallons of milk festering away in gigantic vats, we'd be left with great churns of cream turning into old socks before our very noses. We were just a couple of kids experimenting for the sake of a laugh and we proved beyond a shadow of a doubt that farming is much more difficult than coping with life in London. The variety of horrendous tasks we had to perform was enormous. Sheep-dipping for example: can you picture me up to my eyeballs in a flock of woolly sheep, trying to de-bug them? No dahling, not my scene at all!

The animals all had names like Anabel and Lulubelle which would have made eating them very difficult. In Wales they have a clever system for sensitive souls such as us, dear reader. If one of your sheep dies you grab it and rush it off to the next farm who make good use of it. When one of theirs cops its lot, it's sent to you. That way you never have the guilty pangs of pouring mint sauce over your own Lulubelle.

───────────── **James Herriot Where Are You Now That I Need You?** ─────────────

There were chickens darting all over the place and occasionally one would get under the wheels of your car and would expire with a calm-shattering squalk. Great creatures, chickens – you just shove any old garbage in at one end and out the other pops an egg, regular as clockwork. We had a double-yolker on the farm who laid the most delicious eggs in the entire world. One day the double-yolk eggs disappeared and we thought that the bird had just decided to take things easy for a while. . .until we went to get the car out of the garage and discovered a brown, pancake-shaped mass of feathers under the back wheel. Do chickens have a heaven, I wonder? I hope so.

One of our cows was due to have little baby cow-ettes once, and so Lee and I took it in turns to sit by her side, waiting for the great event so that we could phone *The Times* and put in an announcement. Days and days and nights and nights passed and the cow just stared at us, growing bigger and bigger all the time. We got more and more weary from keeping this seemingly never-ending vigil, so we popped back to the house for a cup of tea, came back an hour later, and there it was, a tiny baby foal, or whatever they're called. The cow had probably been pleading silently with us for days to naff off so that she could get on with it.

It was a pedigree cow-ette as well, its father having been the Hereford prize-fighting mess. We probably would have got medals for it. If we hadn't eaten it, that is.

In between squashing chickens and delivering animals, I would record my programmes for Radio One and drive miles to Swansea station from where they would be whisked straight to the playback machines at Broadcasting House for editing out the naughty bits. The tape often arrived with only moments to spare before it was due for transmission. I used to give the Beeb people heart attacks regularly. Not out of a sense of mischief but I was so busy laying eggs and milking sheep that I just lost track of things and got more and more engrossed in nature's lullaby.

There are some very odd characters in Wales, but the weirdest one I came across was the lady who lived quite near us and who, in the heart of the Welsh countryside, had put lino all down her front path and planted plastic roses all around her garden. Don't ask why. I never could pluck up the courage to talk to her.

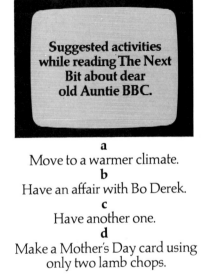

a
Move to a warmer climate.
b
Have an affair with Bo Derek.
c
Have another one.
d
Make a Mother's Day card using
only two lamb chops.

AU REVOIR, AUNTIE... AGAIN

was shaken from my countrified petrification one day by an offer from a new commercial station to work for them. Capital Radio was about to go on the air in London, in stereo, and it sounded fun and exciting, a bit like a land-based Pirate radio station. So once again I parted company with the BBC and set about doing a slightly different show, still on tape from my mountain-top hideaway. With the sort of sentence that could only be uttered by a BBC man, my defection to commercial radio was dismissed thus: 'Negotiations for the renewal of Everett's contract have been ended.'

I didn't have a lot to do with Capital in the beginning but I remember an air of excitement about the place in the early days. The Chairman was (Sir) Richard Attenborough who would waft about the building being very show-biz and avuncular, calling everybody dahling for all he was worth. The Managing Director, John Whitney, supplied the pinstripe respectability necessary to launch an expensive venture like a radio station and the Programme Controller was an ex-BBC man, Michael Bukht.

Michael Bukht is the nearest thing to King Kong I've ever seen. He's a great mountain of a bear of a colossus of a man and has a habit of giving unsolicited bear hugs to people by way of greeting. Most of the early days of the station were spent avoiding his hugs. You could always tell those who'd been caught: they were the ones hobbling around, clutching their sides and making appointments with physiotherapists. He also has a ferocious temper and one day stormed into the building in a foul mood. The word went out 'Bukht's boiling!' and the entire staff of the station cowered at their desks as he bombarded his way down the corridor to his office. He grasped the handle to go inside, but some thoughtful person had locked the door. This was the final straw for the explosive Bukht. He stepped back and delivered a hefty karate chop on the wooden door which nearly broke his hand. Then he kicked the door with all his might. As I've said, he's a big bloke and a kick from Michael Bukht is enough to cause irreparable damage to a Polaris submarine; what chance did a flimsy wooden door stand? The sound of the smashing reverberated around the office, swiftly followed by the noise of the entire ceiling caving in round his head. As the dust, plaster, wiring and girders crashed about his ears, he stood there, watched by the quaking assembly of staff who had gathered to witness the event. The last piece of gunge splintered on his shoulders and he just stood there, glaring at us all. Then, without smiling, he shouted: 'Have a Nice Day, damn you!' went inside what was left of his office and slammed the door. . .which promptly collapsed on its hinges and crashed into the rest of the rubble. Always a

This chapter illustrated by Glenn Marshall.

creature of extremes, that afternoon he went out and bought fifty roses which he distributed among the female members of staff by way of apology.

When I first joined Capital, much was made of the fact that they wouldn't try to gag me. I was allowed to say exactly what I wanted to, which was great. . .for a while. After a time of going on the air and being outrageous without any objections from anybody, I began to feel a bit cheated. There was nothing to rebel against; no-one to tick me off if I went over the top. Where was the fun in that? I'd often storm into Bukht's office and say: 'Hey, listen, how dare you not tell me what to do! I'm not going to stand for it, do you hear! Unless someone complains that I should be thrown off the air, I'm going walk out! I've never been so insulted in all my life. Who the hell do you think you are?' It's a funny old business.

Michael and I did have the occasional barney over things, like how much I was being paid, and the fact that the turntables at Capital weren't made of 22-carat gold. The closest he came to actually phoning me from home while I was on the air was one day when he thought I was being boring. Imagine, darlings! Me! Boring on the radio!!

On this occasion, I began the programme by saying that my special guest was going to be Harry Nilsson. Bukht was at home, listening to the programme and what he heard was me talking to Harry. . .but no Harry talking back. I'd ask a question and then there would be a few seconds' silence: no Nilsson. Michael thought this was quite a spiffing wheeze for a couple of minutes, but I went on doing it and after two hours of the programme in which I'd occasionally put a question to the mysteriously absent Harry Nilsson, Michael was going screaming mad, thinking I'd lost my marbles and was really milking a small joke to death. Just as he was reaching for the phone to call the studio and ask what the hell I thought I was playing at, I said: 'Well, that's about it for today, folks. My thanks to today's special guest, Harry Nilsson.' Harry, who had been sitting in the studio for the whole time, only not joining in with the 'interview', said: 'Well, thanks, Kenny, it's been great to be on the show.' Waddya mean, that's silly? What do you think they pay me for?

On another occasion when Michael was listening to my show from the safety of his own home, I announced to the listeners that today's prize would be a Ferrari. All they had to do was phone in, answer a simple question, and they would win a Ferrari. Bukht went white because, unlike in America where they give away cars, yachts, holidays, trips to the Moon, kisses from Sting and other great prizes, we're not allowed to do that in this country because of silly rules laid down by the Independent Broadcasting Authority which governs commercial radio and TV. The maximum prize value you're normally allowed to offer is about 35p. . .and there I was, giving away a Ferrari. I set the competition, asked the listeners to phone in and sat back while telephone exchanges all over London blew a fuse as thousands and thousands of people dialled the Capital number, all desperate for the Ferrari.

Meanwhile, back at the Bukht ranch, his telephone was ringing constantly with people from the IBA, the Managing Director, the Chairman, the Pope, all calling to find out what the blazes did I think I was doing. He had to pretend he knew exactly what was happening, otherwise he'd appear to be a dummy. . .in short, the whole of London was getting its collective knickers in a twist while I was sitting happily, in a little studio in Euston Tower, enjoying the chaos. . .and all for a Dinky Toy!!

For the first six months or so of its time on the air, Capital pursued a new, adventurous music policy in order to try and give London listeners a real alternative to the BBC, who in 1973 were playing Gary Glitter and the Bay City Rollers until they were coming out of your ears. Capital went for classy music and lots of album tracks which pleased some people, but not enough to make the station a viable proposition.

Capital's early days coincided with the Three Day Week which is probably the worst time you could possibly start a radio station dependent on advertising for its income. When the economy is bad, the first thing to get slashed are company advertising budgets, and we were hit very hard. So hard in fact, that there were rumours floating around that we were on the verge of collapse and that letters informing the staff the party was over had already been typed and were about to be sent. But Sir Dickie-pooh took a Rembrandt or two off his wall and hocked it, and a group of Canadian investors came along to save the day, so the station went on from strength to strength to become the most popular station in London.

───────────────────── **On The Move Again** ─────────────────────

I was sending my weekly Capital show to London in much the same way as I had done for the BBC. Things might have carried on like that for some time to come, but the first set of audience figures for Capital were rather disappointing and I was asked by Michael Bukht to come to London and do the breakfast show.

With a radio station, if you don't grab a big audience first thing in the morning you're sunk, because that's where the biggest potential is in terms of people available to listen. Bukht figured that Everett at breakfast-time might work, and so I was offered large cheques and the use of a house in St John's Wood, where I could live rent-free, all expenses paid, in considerable, centrally-heated comfort.

The call came through on a day when I'd just been shovelling the bull's mess around and been severely gored around the nether regions, so I was not terribly anxious to stick around in the Welsh mud any longer than was strictly necessary. Conditions on the farm had lost their novelty and the thought of being surrounded by a bunch of flamboyant show-biz types, within easy reach of hot and cold running restaurants and cinemas seemed highly attractive.

Not that we gave up the country for ever. After we'd resettled in London and found a buyer for the farm, we decided to buy another place in rural parts, but not quite so far away from civilization this time. We chanced upon a dream house in a little Cotswold village called Little Cherington. The house had belonged to Hugh Griffith the actor, and was a former pub, the Old Red Lion.

Hugh had been matey with Richard Burton who had often come to stay at the house, bringing with him Elizabeth Taylor, so when we moved in I was thrilled to bits to be sleeping in the same bed in which Liz Taylor had kipped, and to be placing my watch on the same bedside table which had once groaned under the weight of her jewellery and false teeth. I'm easily impressed.

There was an inglenook fireplace in the living-room that we'd snuggle into but the house wasn't entirely cosy: there was definitely a ghostly presence. Bosie, our Great Dane, would often turn and bark at a chair just to the left of the fireplace, and his barking would always be preceded by a sudden chill in the air, as if someone had opened a door and let in a draught of air.

Lee had just become interested in spiritualism and mediumness, and one day she got fed up with the barking which was interrupting something we were watching on TV, so she said to the empty chair: 'Look, this isn't a pub anymore, it's a private house and you're upsetting the dog and us, so would you please find somewhere else to visit.' And that was the last time we felt the chill, and the last time Bosie got worked up about that chair.

I think it was the atmosphere of the house which set Lee off on her mediumship. It was one of those very old, low-beamed places with a million nooks and crannies per square inch. She and a friend, Mary, began to get more and more interested in contacting the dead and I'd often return home after a day spent slaving over a hot turntable to discover them having a cosy chat with Henry the Eighth or Guy Fawkes. I tried to join in a couple of times but couldn't really get as enthusiastic about it as the girls. I just couldn't seem to feel whatever it was they were feeling.

Years earlier we'd had a go at the old round-the-table séance routine, with little squares of paper spelling out the alphabet in a circle and a glass in the middle on which we all placed one finger and tried to summon up the spirits. The lights were low and the room was very quiet. There was Lee, myself and a couple of people who worked in television.

The glass began to buzz around the table and spelt out the name of the girlfriend of the cameraman and told us that she was lying dead, in an infirmary. We'd been in the house, the four of us, for a couple of days with no contact from the outside world, no visitors, no phone-calls, and suddenly we all began to feel very spooky about the whole experience. The cameraman telephoned his girlfriend's father to discover that the girl had died that very day.

Bedtime Story

The routine of doing a breakfast show is very gruelling. To be bright and sparky on the air at 6.30 every morning means that you should be asleep by about 10 o'clock every night, especially if you need as much sleep as I do. The problem was that I like to party and boogie when I'm in London, and I got more and more mixed up about what time of day and night it was.

I'd been using sleeping pills on and off for years, but now I became altogether too dependent on the things. I'd take one at about 7 o'clock in the evening, a pill called Mandrax which they don't make any more, thank heaven. The pill would make me buzz before it started to send me off to sleep, so I'd think: 'Hey, let's party,' and I'd have a drink or six which mixed with the pill and made me stagger around in a state of unconscious awakeness until about four in the morning. At 5.30 I'd have to get up and an hour later I'd be sitting in the studio, trying to wipe the glue out of my brain in order to be able to function properly.

Sleeping pills have a cumulative effect on your brain, making you more and more groggy as time goes on. I didn't notice what they were doing to my health until much later, after I'd nearly met with disaster. What happens is that you get

exhausted, but the next pill makes you fly a bit before it knocks you out. When you wake up the next day, the pill is still working inside your system, but it's not functioning as a sleeping pill, just a slowing-down pill. You don't notice how tired you are, because you're half asleep the entire time and that becomes your normal state.

A year or so of constant Mandrax did me no good at all. My brain started to wander all over the place leading to mistakes that I wasn't even aware I was making. I'd introduce records that weren't there, forget appointments, forget names (even more than usual) and think I'd finished doing jobs which I hadn't even started. To wake myself up for the show, I tried cycling to the studio in Euston which, although about three feet lower than St John's Wood, was still a very hard slog. I'd arrive exhausted and hardly be able to open my mouth, let alone be wacky!

Now that we had the place in the Cotswolds, I'd spend the week at the house in London and potter off for some fresh air every weekend. Lee was buzzing back and forth between Little Cherington and St John's Wood, and one night when she was away and I was in a sort of Mandrax haze, I had a go at doing myself in.

Snap, Crackle. . .Flop

Doing the breakfast show can get very depressing. I was either up until all hours which left me feeling exhausted and debilitated, or I would go to bed very early and miss out on all the social whirl. Either way it seemed I couldn't win and I resorted more and more to the little sleeping pills to blot out the depressions, which, as I've said, resulted in a vicious circle of gloom.

One night I took my usual couple of pills and, as they began to take effect and turn my brain into blancmange, it suddenly seemed like a good idea to take another one. . .then another and then another. After the first three, the reasons for staying alive seemed to become blurred and the thought of popping my clogs didn't seem to matter. I was in a sort of woolly world where even the thought of dying didn't seem to matter. Death seemed to be simply the next step. I popped a handful into my mouth and lay there, semi-conscious, waiting for the pearly gates to come into view.

But then I did something which seems to indicate that at the back of my depressed, suicidal, don't-give-a-damn brain was a survival instinct struggling to get out. I phoned Aidan Day, who was then Capital's Head of Music, and said goodbye. I probably told him that I was committing suicide, but I just wanted to say goodbye – I don't remember what I said.

Aidan rushed round with an army of ambulances and I was taken to The Royal Free Hospital in Hampstead. When I woke up the next day the first thing I

saw was a big, white, fluffy shape in front of me which I took to be an angel.

'Oh,' I thought. 'It worked. I'm in heaven. I suppose St Peter will be popping along in a moment to fill out the necessary forms.'

I tried to speak, but the control mechanism for my brain was gunged up with the Mandrax blancmange and nothing came out of my mouth. I just lay there watching, big, cloudy lumps floating about in front of my eyes. Of course, when my focus came back, I discovered that the angels were in fact doctors and nurses. I felt horribly embarrassed at inconveniencing the hospital staff, who have a million better things to do than look after people who've pumped their stomachs full of drugs. But it wasn't my intention to inconvenience anybody. If my plan had worked, I would just have been a job for the undertakers.

While my stomach was being pumped, some kind soul at the hospital had thoughtfully informed the Press of my 'accident'. As you can imagine, though, after an experience like that, the first thing I wanted to do was give a Press conference! But reporters were weasling in and out, all trying to get an interview; in the end my agent, Jo, arranged for me to be smuggled out of the hospital via the laundry lift.

Lee and Jo took me back to the St John's Wood flat and deposited me in bed where I slept for about three days while the Press put us under siege. I'm told that at one point there were about twenty-five reporters phoning, hanging around outside and ringing the bell. Finally Jo disconnected the bell and went out to tell the reporters that I wasn't dead but understandably in no fit state to talk to anyone. To convince them that all was 'as well as could be expected,' she borrowed one of the photographer's cameras and took a photo of me staring groggily into the lens, and it was her picture they used in the papers the following day.

I'd had a fairly similar experience years before when I'd taken too much LSD and had seen my life flash before me, like you're supposed to just before you die. It actually happened: in the space of probably only a few seconds I whirled through an action replay of all that had been, I 'saw' God and Our Lady, worked out the meaning of life and went back to being a baby inside the womb. When I came to, I thought I was in heaven because everything was soft and woolly and the room was filled with all my friends. I thought: 'Well, how lovely – heaven's a beautiful room, filled with all my nearest and dearest. But hang on, what's that telephone doing over there? Why on earth do we need telephones in heaven?' I said to one of the people there: 'So this is heaven, is it?' 'No,' he replied, 'Paddington.'

─────────── **Amazing Fact No 74: Your Brain Is Like The Post Office** ───────────

After my suicide bid-ette I decided, naturally enough, that sleeping pills were not a good idea. The thing that put me off more than anything was a piece I read in a little pamphlet called *Sleeping and Not Sleeping* which Lee found in a chemist's shop. The basic message was that, although it seems easy and convenient to be able to switch yourself off at a certain time every night, what actually should happen when you go to sleep naturally is that all the thoughts from the day and all the plans for tomorrow have to be filed away and put in the right pigeon-holes in your brain, rather like a Post Office sorting department. When you take a sleeping pill, it knocks out the mechanism in your brain which needs to do the sorting. So there's a little man in your head, if you like, who's trying to be neat and tidy and put everything in its proper place but, because of the drug, he can't do his job properly.

All the thoughts from yesterday stay in a disorganized heap on the floor of your mind and, when you wake up the next day, instead of feeling refreshed and renewed and ready to get on with Life, nothing's been put away and you carry scrambled thoughts around with you until the Sorter gets an opportunity to do his job. So you can imagine what a mass of disorganization your brain becomes if you're on sleeping pills for years at a time, like I was.

When I came off the pills, I had three months of nightmares. For the first week I couldn't sleep at all; I just stared at the ceiling. When I did eventually manage to nod off, I dreamt I was awake, staring at the end of the bed where there was a woman with straggly hair and razor-sharp teeth, eating her way up my feet, legs and body. . .aaargh! I'd suddenly wake and sit up in bed shaking and shivering, trying to separate the bog in my brain from what was actually happening.

It took about six months before I got a good night's sleep, but when natural sleep finally took over and swept the remnants of seven years of Mandrax out of my head, it was wonderful! In the days of pills and too much booze and a mass of strange substances coursing through my veins, I'd wake up and the slightest thing would upset me for the whole day. If the temperature was one degree away from perfect, or if the milk was off, I'd become highly argumentative and impossible to live with.

Drugs also lower your resistance to illness and I'd get sick very easily: any bug that was knocking around would have a field day with my innards. And I also used to get paranoid and imagine that people were after me. That's a side-effect common to a lot of drugs, but particularly cocaine. One night when I was stoned on coke, I went with some friends to a restaurant and all through the meal (which I didn't eat – coke suppresses the desire to eat) I assumed that everyone was making jokes at my expense and that they all only wanted to know me because I was on the telly. Then I got to imagining that there was a plot to undermine my self-confidence and my career.

Friends would nag at me to go easy on cocaine, but when you're on it, everyone who isn't seems like a bore and the last thing you want to hear is nagging reminders about how bad it is for you. Your pusher takes over as your best friend, and he, obviously, isn't going to preach the evils of whatever drug is making him rich.

These days I don't take drugs at all. I've come pretty close to disaster through using them and am happy to say that I'm much better off without them. There's nothing worse than a reformed character preaching away, I know, so I'll simply say that if you try and rely on drugs, there's only one word to describe you – sucker.

Me And The Queen – Now It Can Be Told!

I now sleep better and also have great dreams! Often I dream about meeting the Royal Family. I've a great admiration for the whole lot of them – they seem to be *the* example of a very tough job being done to perfection.

I once dreamt I was sitting on a grass verge outside Buckingham Palace, nattering to the Queen.

'It must be a real thrill,' I said to Her Maj.

'For you to be talking to me.'

'Why?' she said.

'Well, you're used to talking to Earls and Viscounts and Captains of Industry. It must be great to meet someone really ordinary like me.'

I don't remember her reply. It was probably something like: 'Off with his head.'

I've never been asked over to the Palace, but I'm expecting an invitation any day now. My three ambitions are to do *Desert Island Discs*, have a cuppa at Buckingham Palace and be pounced upon by Eamonn Andrews with his big red book.

Actually, I tell a lie. I'd hate to be This Is Your Lifed. They've approached both Lee and my Mum to try and nab me but fortunately I've been forewarned, because they know I'd hate it. I've given all my friends strict instructions that if ever an approach is made, I'm to be informed immediately, because obviously they can't do the show if the subject is in on it. Maybe I'm a killjoy, but I can imagine nothing worse than being suddenly confronted with a stageful of people from twenty years ago. I like to get on with things, not hark back to the past.

I was roped in when Eamonn did Michael Aspel's life. They asked me to go on and rave about him, which is not difficult because he's great. I suspected that his attitude towards the whole thing would be much the same as mine but things had gone so far that it wouldn't have been fair to the telly people to let the cat totally out of the bag, so I tried to warn him discreetly.

I saw him at Capital one day about a week before Eamonn was due to pounce and I said: 'I read in your horoscope the other day that you should prepare for a big shock on Monday.' Of course, he didn't have a clue what I was talking about and when it came to the recording of the show, all I could do was tell my silly tale and look apologetically at him.

There now follows a message for any *This Is Your Life* researcher reading this book: '*! *!*!! off please, and turn your attentions to someone else.'

Not Another Word About Eamonn, But More About. . .

. . . poor old Aspel! My old programme on the BBC used to precede him doing that *Two Way Family Favourites* thingy, when they linked up with other radio stations all over the world and sent messages from one family to another. I used to tease him mercilessly towards the end of my show by building him up as a great mincing queen, all draped in lace and dripping with diamonds.

'Oh, here she comes,' I'd say. 'Michael Aspel is wandering into the studio here at Broadcasting House, and he's carrying a beautiful new handbag, made of lettuce leaf, with a diamanté and radish-encrusted tiara tilting fetchingly over his left eyebrow. What a lovely new frock, Michael, where did you get it?'

On and on I'd go, getting more and more outrageous as the weeks went by. Under normal circumstances he would have been able to put me in my place with a well-chosen word, but he wasn't allowed to refer to anything that I'd said. The reason was that my show only went out on Radio One, but, when *Two Way Family Favourites* came on, the transmitters of dozens of radio stations all over the place would click into the Beeb and begin broadcasting Michael's programme. So, as most of his listeners wouldn't have been able to hear me sending him up, he was forced to listen to my tirade of nonsense and then, when the pips went to signify the end of my programme and the beginning of his, all he could do was come on and say: 'The time in Germany is three o'clock, in Hong Kong it's nine o'clock, but all over the world it's time for *Two Way Family Favourites*. . . .'

Poor swine. He put up with this for ages, week in and week out, and simply wasn't allowed to retaliate. He finally got his own back on me on the last day I was handing over to him by reading a poem he'd written which tore me to pieces and which he prefaced by explaining to the listening millions who couldn't hear me that he'd been sent up rotten for years and couldn't allow me to get away with it without having a moment of revenge.

A few years later I was able to send him up again because, while I was doing the breakfast show on Capital, he did the programme which came immediately after mine and so I dragged out all the old lines. This time, however, he was able to retaliate and, more often than not, he won the battle of abuse because he was able to have the last word and then switch off my microphone.

―――――――――――――― **Captain Kremmen And The Coke Factory** ――――――――――――――

After the Battle of the Mandrax, I received a lovely letter from Capital's Chairman, Sir Dickiepooh Attenborough: not merely a letter, but a *handwritten* letter telling me that I should take off as much time as I liked and come back whenever I was ready.

I took his advice and, when I did go back to work, I decided that the breakfast show had been a contributory factor to my lack of health and mental balance, so I did a weekend show instead, into which I introduced a silly space serial starring a new superhero, Captain Kremmen! I'd always been a fan of Dan Dare and all the other inter-galactic adventurers and wanted to invent my own character, who'd be useful for lots of jokes and silly situations.

I used to record it on Friday nights, just hours before it was due to be broadcast at lunchtime on Saturday. I'd had the studio installed in the house in the Cotswolds, and every Friday night I would go there and write out the situations. 'The Captain is trapped inside his spaceship by a man-eating blancmange.' I'd then phone a couple of friends and ask if they knew any man-eating blancmange jokes and work them into the script.

On Saturday mornings I'd get up at seven o'clock, shower and have a cup of coffee and then dive into the studio with my script and piles of sounds effects and knit the whole thing together. Then, at 10.25 precisely, I'd dive into the car and scoot down the M40, arriving just in time to park and fling my bum on the studio chair about thirty seconds before the show was due to start.

On occasions I'd be late and be stuck in a traffic jam listening to the DJ before me making excuses for my non-appearance. I always like to cut things fine, as I've said, but I tend to cause near heart-attacks in those who work with me. Captain Kremmen would be broadcast at about ten past one, and, because I'd only just finished it myself, it seemed fresh and fairly amusing to me too. Kremmen became quite popular, and the radio serial led to a strip cartoon, tee shirts, books and even a regular spot on TV. But cocaine was to blame for the fact that he's now more or less disappeared.

For a while I did short episodes of Captain Kremmen's adventures for Capital's breakfast show which was presented by Mike Smith. Unfortunately, doing this coincided with the period when I was using cocaine rather heavily, and I got more and more interested in the drug and in partying, and less and less concerned about my work. I'd often snort a lot of coke, then go dancing and partying until the small hours. When I got home I still had to do the episode of the space serial for broadcasting only about four hours later at ten past eight. The last thing I wanted to do while I was stoned on coke was to work, so I'd dash off a quick, very sub-standard episode which would often only last thirty seconds and phone a mini-cab to take it to Capital.

I really lost interest in doing any work and it got to the stage where I was so anxious to get the work over and carry on partying that I'd do a script which went something like: 'You remember yesterday's episode. . .you don't? Well, what's the point in doing this one? Stay tuned for more adventures tomorrow.' Really embarrassing in retrospect, and all due to my love affair with little lines of white powder. I knew things were getting really bad when I heard Mike Smith broadcast the episode one morning and then say: 'How much are we paying for this?' That struck home because I knew it was true.

My departure from Capital was amicable. Most of the time when you read that so-and-so is leaving somewhere 'amicably', you can bet that there's been a series of almighty rows and wranglings leading up to the 'mutual decision to part company'. But mine really was 'amicable'.

I was still quite enjoying doing a weekly show for the station, but the buzz that I need to keep me fresh had gone. The worst thing in the world for me is the feeling that I'm in a rut, and after a while I began to function as though I was on automatic pilot, which is no way to present a radio programme. At one stage, shortly before I left, I was doing a three-hour programme once a week, the last hour of which was called 'The Soft Spot' and was a collection of lilting, gentle tunes. . .nice for the audience, but it put me to sleep and at the end of the programme I'd have to make a gigantic effort to rouse myself and make way for the next DJ.

You can tell how much I'd lost interest in radio by the fact that I used to take a bottle of wine into the studio and open it towards the end of the programme. That would give me something to look forward to during the first two hours, and it made the last hour scoot by. The problem was that, as my enthusiasm waned, I began to open the bottle earlier and earlier during the show and, towards the end of my Capital stint, I'd start drinking wine about ten minutes after the start: this produced a slurgy programme and became known as the only wireless show ever to have failed the breathalyzer!

Quite often, after the programme, there would be a journalist waiting to do an interview for a magazine or a newspaper. Me, my producer and the journalist would troop around to the local pub and sit over a Bloody Mary while I told my life story for the umpteenth time. I can never understand why journalists want to do interviews with me, then come along and ask the same questions I've been asked a million times over the years. Surely they could just go to their cuttings library and dig out all the old interviews and glue them together into a new one? In future, when people ask to do interviews I'll just tell them to read this book: it's all in here, folks.

At the time I left Capital I was working very hard on the TV *Video Show* and also making a lot of money doing voice-overs for TV and radio commercials, so I really wasn't desperately keen to work all week, then spend Friday evenings locked in my studio at home, preparing bits for the Saturday radio show, get up at the crack of noon on Saturday and spend two whole hours being wacky on t'wireless. The combination of lethargy and the temporarily healthy state of my bank balance meant that I could afford to give up one area of work, and it seemed natural to stop doing radio for a while.

CASCADES
OF
WEETABIX

Working in television you get a constant conflict between the glamour and excitement, of which there's a teaspoonful, and the annoyance and nerviness of the whole business, of which there is a fridgeload.

Actually doing the bits in front of camera is lovely and jolly and exciting, but the preparations can be exhausting. Armies of make-up girls, technicians, cameramen, sound engineers, directors, tea ladies . . . all rushing around doing bits and pieces in order to get the show together. You have a make-up call for, say, five o'clock and afterwards there's nothing for you to do for two hours, so you have to spend the time sitting around, twiddling your doobries. Another army of people scrabble around with bits of paper and microphones which they pin in the most uncomfortable places and which almost invariably fail just before you go on to do your bit.

It takes hours and hours to get a minute's worth of screen time written, rehearsed and in the can. A half-hour programme like the *Kenny Everett Video Show* took two days of studio work to get the bits involving me onto tape. That, of course, doesn't include the writing, the planning, researching, wardrobe-making and all the other bits that go on before. Nor did it include the dance sequences or routines with musicians and singers. I'd estimate that it takes about a thousand man-hours for one half-hour show.

I mentioned voice-overs a while ago. The terrible truth about them is that when you see a TV commerical, or hear one on the radio, the voice you hear is that of a man or woman who's spent a morning in a dingy little Soho basement extolling the virtues of whatever it is the advertising agency is working on. If you're sensationally professional (like me) the job can be done in about three minutes flat, and, for those three minutes, the cheque is something in the region of £350, plus a fee each time the commercial is screened! Now do you see why all sorts of legitimate actors, such as Peter Barkworth, Robert Powell and Penelope Keith can often be heard telling you all about how fab Nurdlesoup is?

The best money of all, if you're lucky enough to be in this silly business, is doing a commercial when you're actually seen on-screen. For a day's work in a studio, grinning stupidly at a camera while holding up a pack of Nurdlesoup, you can get as much as £10,000, often more if you're someone really stupendously famous. If I'm lucky, I might get two or three of those a year and, needless to say,

This chapter illustrated by Malcolm Harrison.

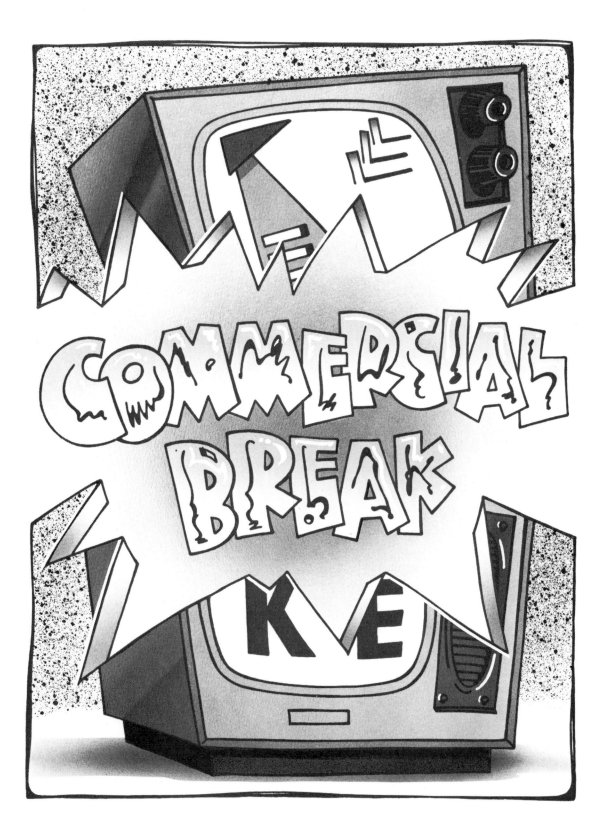

I'm delighted to be asked. As well as being wonderfully well-paid, they're also quite fun to do. Everyone's keen to get the best out of you and so they treat you like royalty for a day. Mind you, as far as I'm concerned, the promise of the large cheque at the end of the day is enough to make me give wall-to-wall smiles for as long as they like.

One of the first TV commercials I ever did was for Picnic Bars. It was in the days before I became fairly well-known, and so I was asked to do a test commercial to see if I was any good. I held up a Picnic Bar to the camera and burbled my way through a very dreary script about how nice Picnic Bars tasted because they were filled with quite nice crunchy bits and covered with chocolate. It really was deathly-dull so, at the end of what they wanted me to do, I asked them to keep the camera running and just launched into my own ad-lib thirty-second routine, saying something like: 'This bar . . . is the only bar of chocolate with Queen Anne legs . . . it's got knobbly bits on the side . . . and just look at those scrumbly, wurdly, oodgilie-woodgilie lumps . . . ooh, you'll go potty-poos. . . .'

They loved it. They threw away the original script and I did a whole load of wacky blurbs about knobbly bars of chocolate which the client, Mr Picnic, adored. We did one where I was supposed to say something on these lines: 'There are so many knobbly, bulgy, crunchy bits in a Picnic Bar that it won't stand up on its end! Stand it on its end and . . . look! . . . it falls over. *And* it's only sixpence!' The problem was that, when we went into the studio to film this advert, every single Picnic Bar we had (and we had hundreds) refused to fall over! We had to cheat by inserting a round-headed screw into the bar; we put it on the table, and then someone crawled underneath with a magnet which he yanked away at the appropriate moment. What a way to make a living, I hear you cry. How right you are!

As I write, my house is over-run with packets of Weetabix. I did a commercial for them a while ago and cheekily said: 'Oooh, I love Weetabix, why don't you send me a crate, darling!' (Cheek always works, and anyway, it wouldn't have been the end of civilization as we know it if they hadn't taken the hint.) The next day two enormous crates of Weetabix arrived. I had about two packets myself and now, whenever I go to a party, instead of taking a bottle I present my hostess with her very own pack of individually-wrapped Weetabix. Come to think of it, the invitations *have* been a little thin on the ground recently. . . .

Apart from a lifetime's supply of Weetabix, the other jolly perk about appearing on TV is that Thames or the BBC give you a clothes allowance so, from time to time, I nip off to a shop, wander round and say: 'I'll have that, that, that, six of those, a dozen of those, three of those and a pair of those.' And then they send the bill to the TV company!

When the *Video Show* was taking off and I was picking up three or four awards every ten seconds, I had to keep going to Moss Bros to hire suits which I hated because they were prickly and very uncomfortable. So I went off to another tailor near Piccadilly and had an elegant suit made up at vast expense and had the bill sent to Thames . . . which was a bit cheeky because the following day I wore it on the BBC when I was on Michael Parkinson's show! I've still got the suit and it's the only one I feel comfortable in because it's brown and squashy and it looks as though I've been dipped in a big vat of hot chocolate.

The other guests on the Parky show were John Curry, the ice-skater, who was sweet but rather shy, and Bob Geldof of the Boomtown Rats who was quite content to mumble, tell one joke and let me steal the rest of the show which I did with the help of a bunch of silly gimmicks I'd bought earlier in a shop, like tennis balls which you wind up and let them walk all over the table. I also brought on a box which said 'Golfer's ball-cleaning set' which contained a jock-strap with a scrubbing brush attached. Props are very handy on a TV chat show, especially if you're a scene-stealer, like me! Chat-shows are more fun to do than newspaper interviews because the nerves surrounding television make you perform a bit better and, of course, you're playing to a live studio audience which means you try harder to get laughs.

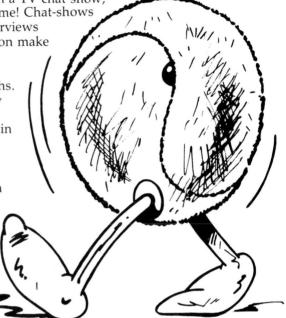

I was once on the Russell Harty show with Janet Street-Porter and, after about two minutes, it became clear that in the scene-stealing stakes I was just a beginner when put up against her, so I gave up and sulked in a corner.

When I went to New Zealand a while ago, I went on a TV chat show. One of the other guests was Julie Goodyear, Bet Lynch from *Coronation Street*. They show the programme in New Zealand but they're about three years behind us, so I couldn't resist the temptation to tell the whole of the country what was going to happen in the next three years of The Street. Sorry, NZ, but just think of all the time I've saved you. You can now spend three extra years' worth of half-hours frolicking on the beach and throwing up your Fosters!

Another TV appearance which seems to have gone down quite well is the time I appeared on a regional TV programme hosted by a man who'd become nationally famous after one of his interviews had been screened on Denis Norden's *It'll Be All Right On The Night*. The interviewer had been talking to a man who kept ferrets and one of the nasty little beasts had jumped out of the keeper's control and sunk its teeth into the poor interviewer. It was rather like the time when Rod Hull/ Emu attacked Parkinson, only this time it was for real and the razor-like teeth were digging into this poor man's hand and there was nothing he could do to make it let go. He writhed around for a few moments, wrestling with the ferret and won the hearts and adulation of a million viewers.

We talked about this and that in usual chat-show style and, about thirty seconds before I knew my time was up, I said: 'You know you're very famous, don't you?' 'No,' he said, 'why is that?' 'Yes,'I said, 'the whole country knows you.' He was genuinely puzzled. 'Well, that's very flattering, but I can't imagine why.' 'This is why,' I said and leapt on him, sank my teeth into his hands and refused to let go until the end of the show.

There are, understandably, people who believe that everything they see on TV is happening as they're watching it . . . well, not everything. I think most people have cottoned on to the magic of pre-recording, but I'm sure there's still a hard core of little old ladies who are convinced that newsreaders learn the news off by heart before cleverly insinuating themselves into little boxes in the corner of the living-room. Most programmes are, of course, pre-recorded so that any mishaps can be edited out before transmission. Not so in the case of a series of chat-shows hosted by Russell Harty.

Now, doing a live programme in front of millions is nerve-racking and nail-biting enough as it is. Inviting me to appear on that programme is a sort of modern-day equivalent of Hara-Kiri (or do I mean Biryani?). Russell Harty was once daft enough to invite me to appear on his show, and before the programme started I told him that I was feeling just a touch mischievous and that I intended to recite a poem which began:

'The boy stood in the chip shop,
Eating red hot scollops. . .'

I told him no more than that but the sweat glistened on his forehead all through the show as he tried to convince himself that nobody, not even Cuddly Ken, could be so cruel . . . surely not. The show progressed and I wackied and zanied away in my usual manner. Then, just towards the end, I saw the floor manager 'counting him down' to the end of the programme.

'Thirty seconds to go,' came the signal.

Suddenly I interrupted Russell's closing spiel.

'Hey,' I yelled, drowning out his voice. 'I've got a poem!'

Russell went green.

'Twenty seconds to go.'

'The boy stood in the chip shop,
Eating red hot scollops,
One fell down his trouser leg [pause for effect]
. . . . and scalded his ankles.'

As Russell breathed a Force Nine gale of relief and the final credits began to roll over the applause of the studio audience, I shouted the punch-line:

'. . . missed his bollocks completely!!'

It was too late for my poor, bemused host to say or do anything but grace the camera lens with one last despairing grimace and then the screen went dead, leaving the announcer to pick up the pieces with the usual sugar-plum fairy voice: 'This is BBC2. . . .'

Sorry, Russell. Well, sorry-ish.

―――――――――――――――――――― **Good Old Reliable Kenny** ――――――――――――――――――――

There used to be a TV programme called *Celebrity Squares* which was a copy of an American game show called *Hollywood Squares*. A bunch of well-known people were plonked in a stage of noughts-and-crosses boxes and were asked daft questions by Bob Monkhouse. My job on the show was to sit in a little booth at the back of the control room and, whenever a little red light came on in the booth, reel off a list of prizes in a wacky voice. Hardly the most taxing job in the world, but the money was good and it was a bit of a laugh. Every week Jo Gurnett, my agent, and I would trundle off to what was then ATV and sit in a little dark room with a script and a bottle of brandy. There we'd sit playing Scrabble while the show was being taped, waiting for my cue-light to flicker.

One day Jo and I were sitting in our little hideaway, waiting for the programme to start, and we were watching the audience come in and the celebrities taking their positions in their boxes. We were chatting about a TV advertisement we'd seen recently which featured a man dressed as a superhero. He was a fine specimen of the human physique, and his costume had been specially designed to make him look super-hunky, with particular attention paid to his crotch area. I said something like: 'Hey, he looks as though he's got a bunch of bananas hidden in his trousers.' There was a sudden gale of laughter from the studio audience. The microphones in the booth had inadvertently been switched on and our conversation about this man's bulge was echoing through the studio. The audience laughter was heightened by the fact that, as I said the bit about the bananas, Bob Monkhouse walked onto the stage and everyone assumed I was talking about him. After that there was no conversation in the booth. We played Scrabble in silence and I only spoke when the cue-light flashed on.

Anyone who's worked with me will tell you that, while I might be one for cutting things fine, I always turn up eventually (well, with a couple of exceptions). My agent says that I've become more reliable over the years which is probably because, as I grow older, I tend to feel more responsible about what I do and I realize that if I'm late for a show, it holds up dozens of other people unnecessarily.

On one occasion I was late for *Celebrity Squares*, for a legitimate reason, but they all thought I'd just been lazing about. Jo and I were on our way to ATV to do the recording when we were involved in a rather nasty car crash. A car pranged into my BMW and very nearly wrote it off. The driver was screaming and shouting at me for all he was worth. All he had was a slightly dented bumper but somehow my car was a crumpled heap. After exchanging names and addresses with the other lunatic, I managed to phranurdgle down to the studio and hurled myself into my little sound-booth seconds before the red light came on, and then had to go into a wild 'n' wacky routine about a holiday of a lifetime which was the star prize of the show. The producer was cross because he thought I was exaggerating about the car crash, and I had to take him to the car park to show him the wreckage before he'd calm down.

So, while I really am quite good at being where I'm supposed to be, thanks to the super organization of my life by Jo, there have been occasions when I've slipped up. A while ago I was due to take part in a television programme which London Weekend Television was recording with Dudley Moore. I was scheduled to be among the studio audience and, at some point during the show, I was supposed to stand up and ask him a question. Jo fixed up all the details and arranged the tickets for me and some friends, but she couldn't actually accompany me to the studio herself. A couple of weeks after the show had been recorded she asked me how I'd enjoyed the Dudley Moore evening. I hadn't enjoyed it at all . . . because I'd completely forgotten all about it and had happily sat watching an old movie on TV. Sorry about that, Dud, but the audience was filled with celebrities asking questions anyway, so I don't suppose for a moment that I was really missed.

On another occasion I was due to make a guest appearance on a Thames programme called *Afternoon Plus*, but I got the times muddled up. At 2.30 I happened to phone Jo about something and she said: 'How can you be calling me from a live TV studio?' 'I'm not,' I said. 'I'm at home. I'm not due there for half an hour . . . am I?' 'You daft lemon!' screamed Jo, 'I'm watching the programme NOW. The show's just started and they've said you're one of the guests!!' At this point Jo's other line rang and it was Thames TV politely asking where the *!***!**! hell was Kenny Everett??? The answer was that I was screaming through heavy lunchtime traffic, having left the phone dangling as I dived into the car and set off for the Euston studios. I did actually make it . . . but not until literally twenty seconds before the end of the show. The presenter was just saying: 'Goodbye, see you next time, and we are sorry that Kenny Everett couldn't make it . . .' when I burst into the studio, knocking cameras and technicians flying, and just managed to wave dementedly into the camera before the show was over. The producers were sweet enough to invite me back on the show and they offered to send a car for me . . . and a back-up car to follow behind just in case something went wrong. This time I was at the studio an hour early and sat twiddling my thumbs like a naughty schoolboy.

Once, when I was oh so young, I achieved the almost-impossible of making Tony Blackburn angry. (Yes, folks, it *can* be done!)

He'd invited Lee and myself to dinner, along with his then-wife, Tessa Wyatt, at their house in the country. He explained that the house was a bit tricky to find, but if I turned off at Junction 8 on the M4, all would be revealed and a jolly time had by all. Seven o'clock was the estimated time of arrival and Tony and Tessa had prepared everything and were happily supping a pre-dinner eggnog, waiting for their guests to arrive.

Seven o'clock came . . . seven-thirty . . . eight o'clock . . . eight-thirty . . . nine o'clock . . . ten . . . eleven . . . finally, at midnight with no sign of Lee or myself, Tony took out his teeth, Tessa put their pet sloth out for the night, and they went to bed.

At about twelve-thirty the doorbell rang at the Blackburn residence: there we were, Lee and myself, standing sheepishly in the porchlight, feebly clutching our extremely warm bottle of Frascati.

'Sorry we're late,' I said. 'Got a bit lost.'

'There's lost,' said Tony, 'and then there's *lost*. We were expecting you at seven o'clock. What on earth happened?'

'I missed the turn-off,' I said, giving my Sunday-best smile.

'Well where have you been?' asked Tony.

Lee and I looked at each other, and said, as with one voice: 'Wales.'

We'd driven the entire length of the M4 motorway and only noticed we'd missed the junction when we got to the Toll Bridge which takes you into the Land of the Leek. It just goes to show the lengths to which some people will go in order to avoid dinner with Tony Blackburn!

─────────────────────── **Exploding Violins** ───────────────────────

I'm not very keen on doing things which involve large live audiences. I can't do a stand-up comedy routine, and I'm not the sort of disc-jockey who can arrive at a club and do an hour's personal appearance, just playing dance records. The comfort of sitting in a radio studio, wearing tee shirt and jeans, is something I cherish. Radio lets me build up wonderful pictures, and even though I may be looking and feeling like a hung-over water buffalo, all I have to do is sound sparky and I can get away with it.

Some time ago Ray Cameron organized something called *The Kenny Everett Juke Box* which was a video cassette of stand-up comedians recorded in front of a live audience at a London club. Barry Cryer, John Junkin, Willie Rushton, Lennie Bennett and a number of other professional funny men rehearsed comedy routines which they were to deliver to the audience and my job was to introduce each turn and fill in the bits between the acts. That's about all I can remember about the evening, because the fact that I was appearing in front of a live audience caused my whole brain to turn into a petrified mass of nerve-ends.

A lot of DJs make a great deal of money by doing guest appearances at discos and clubs around the country. For an hour's slot, playing records and giving away tee shirts and stickers, they can pick up anything between £100 and £1,500 depending on their stature and famousness. Much as I like the money, I gave up doing disco appearances years ago. I was in a club one night, doing my bit on stage, when I caught sight of the manager heading for what seemed to be a trouble spot at the other end of the dance floor. Two minutes later I saw him again. This time he was being carried out by two bouncers and there was a broken bottle embedded in his face. That was my last guest appearance at a disco. No money is worth that kind of risk, and anyway, when I'm in a club, I like to boogie and bop the night away and let someone else worry about the records and things.

One of my favourite sketches on the TV shows was very nearly disastrous. You can have no conception of the physical danger in which we delicate performers constantly live and work in our never-ending quest to bring you wacky bits.

I was supposed to be a punk singer, with The Pretenders as my back-up group. At the end of screaming this terrible, raucous song, I was supposed to plunge the microphone through the lens of the camera: this would have been desperately expensive to do for real, so a plate of glass was held in front of the camera and I duly sang the song and thrust my microphone-clutching hand through the glass. When I pulled my hand back, there was a bit missing: blood all over the studio floor and bits of thumb flying around the room.

I was hoiked into a taxi and whisked off to hospital with blood gushing from my wound. I was given stitches on arrival, and if there's one thing I can't stand it's having stitches: it's like somebody knitting a cardigan with your skin. They did it while I was conscious too. I was given a local anaesthetic in my thumb and then sat watching as this massive great javelin was made to sew my dangly hand back together again.

Battle-weary and half-fainting, I was then taken back to the studio to carry on making the programme. The next sketch involved me and an exploding violin. I was to be dressed entirely in black except for my wrists and hands, and I would pretend to play the end of Paganini's Violin Concerto which comes to a nipple-curdling climax. At this point I was supposed to press a button at the bottom of the neck of the instrument which would set off a massive explosion inside the violin. The props guy who designed it must have been having an off-day because what he hadn't realized was, that for me to activate the explosion, my hand would have to be directly over the powder-box. I must have been having an off-day as well, because the danger of what I was doing didn't occur to me either and pretty soon I was whisked off to hospital again, where they patched up my raw, blistered fingers and sent me packing, obviously wondering what on earth I got up to in my spare time.

Whatever it was the doctors did for me didn't work, and when I got home that evening I was in agony and couldn't sleep at all. My fingers felt like lumps of freshly-cooked spare-ribs, so I got a bundle of ice-cubes from the fridge and spent the night with my hand dangling in a bucket of iced water by the bedside. That didn't work either because half my hand was on fire and the other half was like an Arctic Roll, so eventually I called a doctor who came and gave me a jab of some pain-killing stuff which sent me flying sky high, and within ten minutes I was apparently talking about what a nice vet he was and would he like to come to tea and bring some more of his miracle drug?

There really is no formula for what we do on the show but one thing we do strive for is understatement. Take, for example, a sketch we did with Freddie Mercury of Queen. It was called the Eurovision Violence Contest and we brought in Katie Boyle to say: 'And now here's Freddie and Ken with their latest hit.' Cut to Freddie socking me on the jaw. Cut to me smacking him in the teeth. Cut to Katie saying: 'Luxembourg, deux points,' and you've got a jolly thirty-second sketch which contains stars and a fairly strong, throw-away gag. Most other shows would build that up too much and milk about two minutes out of it, which would make it flat. With us, thing are over so quickly that, if something doesn't work 100 per cent, by the time the viewer's decided he doesn't like it, we're off into another completely different idea.

The popularity of the shows I do is obviously important to me. It's nice to know that all the effort we've all put in is paying off and that the shows are being enjoyed by as many people as possible. So I could never understand why, when the telly show was on ITV, they scheduled us against *Top Of The Pops* on the BBC. *TOTP* is an institution: whether or not they do it well doesn't matter – it's still a documentary record of the latest chart hits and that's what most kids are most interested in. It seems daft, therefore, to put a show like mine up against it. If ITV had wanted to use the *Kenny Everett Video Show* as a powerful tool in the ratings war, they should have put it on opposite something completely different, and have offered a real alternative to *TOTP*, like a play or an opera.

Apart from viewing or listening figures, the other gauge of popularity is the string of awards ceremonies which happen every year. Some are more important than others, but my basic philosophy about the whole thing is that if there are awards to be won, it's better to win them than not. Sound thinking, huh?

The point about the whole awards game is that there's a degree of predictability about them. If there's a new sparkly show, it's likely to scoop all the accolades going for its first year, but after that it becomes established and, even though it might be getting better, because it's been around for a while, it's no longer a prime contender. *Not The Nine O'Clock News* was in that position a while ago: they picked up every award going, but even though they've become more polished as they've learned from their mistakes, they're now as much a part of the established set of programmes as *Panorama*, and so they're unlikely to win more prizes. Occasionally, though, the judges will dish out a bit of Perspex-on-a-stick to one of the old-style shows, like *The Two Ronnies*, just to throw a spanner in the works.

It's particularly odd how soon a naughty, off-beat, risqué programme can become part of the Establishment. Think how outrageous *Monty Python* was considered when it first appeared. Now, those programmes are part of the folkweave – the grandads of TV silliness. In a way, it's the spin-offs which tell you that a show is going over the hill. As soon as you bring out a book or a tee shirt to accompany a TV series, you're seen to have almost sold out and you're no longer thought of as being in the vanguard of wackiness.

Come Fly With Me

I've discovered a great knack for surviving long plane journeys: get very drunk and pass out quick. I came across this technique after a terrifying flight in the course of

duty. I was flying to Los Angeles, and I took
with me one of those little Sony Walkman personal
stereo headsets; you know, the ones you see roller-skaters peeling off their heads after
colliding with a juggernaut.

The plane was flying over Las Vegas, just before arriving in LA, and I was
fiddling about with my Sony which has a built-in radio, trying to listen to some
American radio stations as we flew over the transmitters. All very illegal, because it
can interfere with the aircraft's radar, but I didn't know that at the time.

There I was, blissfully bopping away in my seat, when the voice of the pilot
suddenly broke through the radio station and I heard him talking to the control
tower in Los Angeles: 'LA Control, this is Delta Foxtrot Delta. The terrorist on board
has now left a message in the washroom to the effect that the bomb will explode at
21.00 hours. Please have emergency services standing by.'

At first I thought I must have plugged into the in-flight comedy channel, but
pretty soon I realized that the last thing they'd have on a plane would be a sketch
about a plane being blown up in mid-air. This was real! This was happening! There
was a bloody bomb on board MY PLANE!

I turned to my agent, who was sitting next to me, and told her what I'd heard and we did the only thing any normal, self-respecting frightened individuals would do under the circumstances: ordered a bottle of champagne and settled down to get plastered in preparation to meet our Maker.

One of the stewards wandered down the aisle and I beckoned to him and told him what I'd heard. He, of course, told me not to mention anything or to panic and tried to reassure me that the bomber was in fact just a hoaxer. I attempted to believe him, but ordered another bottle of champagne just in case and sat nervously watching the time tick around to 21.00 hours.

At nine-o'clock precisely the sign to fasten seat-belts came on and I was convinced that we were never going to see Los Angeles, never going to ride the wild surf on Malibu, never going to laugh again at Russell Harty's toupee. I gripped the seat as hard as I could and braced myself for the explosion.

At that point I must have passed out from the combination of alcohol and terror because the next thing I knew the plane had landed and we were being asked to sit in our seats and remain there for our own safety. It's the same old line they always give you when you come into land but, somehow, because of the events leading up to our arrival at LA airport, I was doubly convinced that at any moment there would be an almighty bang.

For about half an hour after touchdown we were told to remain seated and, even though the fear was coursing through my veins, there was no point in screaming and shouting because everyone would have become hysterical if they'd realized what was going on and that might have scared the bomber, if there was one, into setting off his device.

Eventually the captain's voice appeared over the intercom and we were asked to evacuate the aircraft as quickly as possible which, strangely enough, I was only too happy to do. The doors opened and the plane was surrounded by police cars. Just like a scene from *Kojak*. We were then ushered into the Customs Hall and after a time we were allowed to leave. We never discovered the end of the story: was there a bomber? Or was it just a hoax? Whichever, the experience provided me with one of the most unforgettable flights of my life, and a good excuse to down two bottles of champagne at breakneck speed. Next time I fly, I'm leaving the Sony machine in my suitcase. If I'm going to go, I'd rather not know about it in advance.

─────────────── **More About Foreign Parts** ───────────────

Lee and I once took a holiday in the Seychelles. When we got to our big, concrete holiday hotel, we decided that we'd rather be in a little hut somewhere and get away from the yards and yards of screaming kids. We left the main island and found a little island-ette called Praslin which was showered with sunshine. We got in the local taxi which took us up a pretty hill to the hotel: it had about six cabins with thatched roofs and slatted windows, no glass. Very picturesque by day – but a living hell by night.

As darkness fell, we'd light a little bug-repelling curly candle doobrie which fizzes all night and keeps the nasties away. I'm not surprised because the smell is revolting, like concentrated Harpic. At nine o'clock the generator would switch off and we were left in this desperately quiet island in the middle of the Indian Ocean. Not a sound to be heard, except for the humming of marauding bugs warming up to re-enact the Battle of Britain right around our hut. They were attracted by the little bedside light which was the only light on the island – everyone else knew that the only way to get a good night's sleep was to turn all the lights off at nine o'clock, but we thought we'd try and read. Mistake! Every insect which had wings, legs, wheels, skates . . . every bug in the Indian Ocean area suddenly converged on our hut! Bugs with short legs, long legs, no legs, furry wings, prickly wings, sticky wings, beady eyes, blinking eyes, no eyes . . . you name it, they came to present their compliments. I jumped out of bed and ran around the room brandishing a copy of the local paper, the Praslin Bugle or whatever, trying to swat this Luftwaffe of insects! Of course, to swat them I had to keep the light on, which only made matters worse because as soon as I'd scored a hit, the dying bug would be replaced by at least ten of its friends.

Eventually I gave up and Lee and I lay huddled together, trying desperately to ignore the dive-bombing attacks which were hitting the other side of the blanket. At about three in the morning there was a noise on the outside of the slatted windows which sounded like a Sherman tank trying to break in. We peered out of the top of the blankets and saw a thing the size of a tortoise flying into the room and heading straight for us. (I'm not exaggerating, it really was that big, and if Hitler had had an army of them, he'd have won the war.) We dived back under the blankets and quivered with fright as we heard this thing clunk to the floor.

Then I had an attack of fearless masculinity and jumped out of bed, preparing for battle. I looked around the room for something big enough to put over it, like a bucket, but there was nothing that would do, so I took a deep breath and picked it up! I put one hand on top of the beast, one hand underneath and tried to keep my hands away from its head which was snapping around, trying to eat my finger. I threw it out on to the grass and fled back to the safety of the bed, where I didn't sleep a wink for the rest of the night. I think Lee must have passed out. The next day we scarpered from the island-ette as quickly as possible and spent the rest of the holiday in air-conditioned comfort, dreaming every night of flying tortoises with teeth the size of
Donny Osmond.

B

illy Connolly is the world's most giggly human being. I've never known anyone enjoy laughing so much as Our Bill. He seems to find something funny in absolutely everything. We were doing a sketch for the telly show once in which I played Fyffe Robertson interviewing Billy who was a lavatory attendant at Waterloo Station.

'What's it like being a lavatory attendant?' I asked, and thrust under his nose a microphone that was a stiff loo chain with a ball on the end.

Billy had to launch into a great tirade about how the loo business had deteriorated over the years; how, in the old days, there used to be a really classy clientele visiting the toilets, all done up in top hats and tails, the height of respectability. Nowadays all you got were junkies and perverts using the lavatories for filthy practices. In fact, these days, when anyone comes in for just an ordinary shit, it's like a breath of fresh air. (Alright, it doesn't look great on paper, but it was funny on t'telly!)

All the way through Billy's lines, we had a stream of people going in and out of the toilet; there was a wrinkly old actor who walked in wearing a blue dress and juggling with fruit, and reappeared a few moments later dressed as a cowboy . . . all sorts of nonsensical things. The problem was that Billy could see what was going on behind him reflected in the glass of the Autocue machine, and every time he caught sight of one of these bizarre characters, he burst out laughing. Not just the sort of giggle that happens quite often, but a real uncontrollable fit of hysteria which took at least twenty minutes to recover from. We tried the sketch three or four times and each time Billy cracked up. It looked as though we wouldn't be able to finish the piece, so we decided that the sight of a giggling, scratty-haired Scot was funny in itself and we included the clips of him laughing uncontrollably in the finished show.

Denis Norden has used that technique of people muffing their lines to great effect with his *It'll Be All Right On The Night* shows. I'm a great fan of Denis, who's been responsible for some of the great lines of our time. I was listening to him on a

This chapter illustrated by Mike Gornall.

radio panel show once. The host of the show asked him to listen to a bit of some raucous, new wave rock band and identify the name of the group and the song. There then followed twenty seconds of hideous screeching and wailing, and Denis said something like: 'I've reached the stage in life when my mind is so completely filled with carefully graded and edited jolly memories that, in order to assimilate any new piece of information, something already in my brain has to go to make way for the new fact. Having just listened to that effrontery to my aural appendages, I can quite safely say that there is nothing – no matter how trivial – which I am prepared to exchange for the information you seek about that piece of noise.' He said it better, of course, but isn't that a lovely way of summing up some of the nasty noises which appear under the name of music these days?

David Essex is another real professional I've worked with from time to time. He's got sparkly eyes, healthy skin, a great head of hair and a good physique. Let me think . . . I know there's some other reason why I can't stand him!

Bernard Manning was a guest on one of the telly shows, and I must confess that I was a bit apprehensive at first because of the image he has: rude and rather unfriendly. I was sure he'd turn out to be a monster to work with, but when we came to film the sketches, he was utterly charming and a complete professional. He stood on the right mark, performed his lines immaculately and was generally very polite and charming.

I did find him a bit odd during the lunch-break, however. My scriptwriters, Barry Cryer and Ray Cameron, and I were nattering on in our usual manner and Manning was sitting at the table like a large but sweet lump of suet pudding. He didn't seem to have any conversation: all he did was tell jokes. We'd be talking about Poland or curries or something intrinsic and important and suddenly this great, gravelly voice would boom out: 'Did you hear the one about two poufs in a lift?' Then a long string of jokes would gush out, which was a bit peculiar after a while; rather like a TV set that had been left on even though no one was watching it.

We came to the conclusion that he only knew jokes, and had no way of communicating in ordinary conversation. Maybe he felt as though he was supposed to perform even with no cameras around. Some entertainers are like that: always 'On'. It's as though they are two different people, the real one and the one we see on TV, but the problem is that they know everyone likes the image they project on the screen, so they retreat behind it at all times, and the real person gets submerged.

David Bowie made a great impression on me the first time I saw him. He was on *The Old Grey Whistle Test* and I thought he looked like a sort of thin, weird Elvis. It was ages before he became a cult, but I remember being knocked out by his style.

He didn't seem to be going through any of the Stage One petty neuroses that most of us do like: 'Will they like me?' 'Am I any good?' 'Help!' He looked as though he just thought: 'Look, I know I'm great so like it or lump it. This is what I do, and it's wonderful.' His brand of strutting self-confidence obviously worked on people, because look where he is today.

You wouldn't think that he'd be amenable to making a fool of himself, would you? He looks all aloof and above it all, but we were delighted when he came on the *Kenny Everett Video Show* years later. We did a silly sketch in which Bowie played the violin and I came on, dressed as Angry of Mayfair, and lambasted him for playing filthy, degenerate, hip-grinding, homosexual, scandalous music and began beating him over the head with my umbrella. He then chased me with the violin bow and began bashing me back and I started pleading for more. Very bizarre, but it was probably the only time anyone has bashed David Bowie over the head and got away alive.

I've been very lucky with the latest batch of television shows. We usually had a star on the programme, singing their latest hit, but instead of just showing a video of them performing we invited them to take part in one or two sketches, so that it looked like they were more a part of the show.

Then there was the time I fulfilled every girl's dream and writhed about with **Sting** of The Police. He had come in to do a song for the show, and while he was there we asked if he'd mind taking part in a silly sketch which only took about 30 seconds to dream up, a minute to put on film and provided many chuckles and fantasies for the audience.

We had **David Frost** on the show a while ago. It's surprising how people you might think would be terribly stand-offish and too image-conscious to make a fool of themselves, aren't at all. All that nonsense about star quality and 'I need my own ocean-going caravan on the set before I'll do anything' has gone out of the window, especially in television where people seem to want to join in for the fun of things. **Cliff Richard, Michael Aspel, Billy Connolly, Terry Wogan** – they've all appeared on my TV shows at some time or other and have come off the set looking like nanas, often dripping with green slime. But they're relaxed enough and sufficiently secure not to mind.

Rod Stewart was a bit odd when he came on. Usually, when you record a pop tune, you just sling up a set, the band come in, do a couple of rehearsals and then do it for real. But Rod took about four hours to do one number; most of the time was spent getting the right camera angles on his bum. Four hours of bum-flinging later, he got the song right and we all went for a drink in the bar. He sat there with his entourage and I sat there with Barry Cryer and Ray Cameron. They were cracking a million great jokes a second and the three of us were rolling around in hysterics. Rod just sat there staring into his brandy and lime, not saying a word. Finally, Barry gave up trying to jolly the party along and said: 'OK, then, let's play "Pass the Parcel".' I think the Rod Mob got the hint, because they got up and walked out.

Maybe Rod suffers from what The Beatles used to go through, which is being expected constantly to perform, but he hasn't developed the protective mechanism of sarcasm which helped keep the Fab Four chortling. He's chosen to surround himself with heavies who deflect anything that could possibly be unpleasant and upsetting.

Elton John is a real sweetiepie. I went to his mansion once. It's a huge place in Virginia Water, and there's a massive TV screen in every room, always on. He was sitting at the piano, just picking out the odd note here and the odd note there. It was lovely to watch, because he'd do it without feeling self-conscious about it, there only being one or two chums around. He would plonk away at the piano for a while and then say: 'Hey, what do you think of this?' And then he'd play the bare bones of what would turn out to be his next hit some months later.

Paul McCartney is another who would try out new tunes on people who were just lolloping around the place. I visited him once in his house in St John's Wood, which I approached through gates made of steel and Alsatian teeth. Once inside, you found that everything was terribly comfortable and beautiful, all painted white with pillars dotted about and a sprinkling of pianos and tape machines in every room. He'd sit around tinkling away, adding a note here and taking away a note there, and then he'd try something out on us which would turn out to be *Hey Jude* or some such monster classic.

Some friends of mine once had Paul round to tea, years ago, and he was sitting around nattering when he said: 'Hey, I've written something this morning. Do you want to hear it?' Of course they all said yes, so he went and got his guitar and played them a little something he'd just jotted down on the back of a fag packet . . . called *Yesterday*.

One day at Paul's place a piano was delivered when I was there. It was a baby grand and, because its new owner was to be Paul McCartney, Bechsteins had sent a concert pianist to tune it up for him. Instead of a little old man going 'Plink, plonk. Yes, that's all right,' the pianist sat down and played the whole of something like Mendelssohn's Piano Concerto in L. Everyone who was in the house sat listening to the virtuoso performance and, when it was finished, the pianto tuner/concert pianist just said: 'Yes, that'll do,' and left.

I was quite friendly with **Brian Epstein** for a while, and was at his place in Belgravia one day with a bunch of people when he asked if we'd like to hear the lastest thing that The Beatles had done. It was just before *Magical Mystery Tour* came out and we sat around his house, feeling privileged beyond belief and listening to *I Am A Walrus* and *Fool On The Hill* before anyone else in the world. Eppy wandered off to bed and everyone else slowly left, so I decided to be extremely naughty and I pinched the tape. The only copy in existence! Imagine what would have happened if I'd been burgled or there had been a fire . . . too horrible to contemplate!

I took the tape home and made a copy of it, then slipped the original back into Eppy's cupboard. I then wandered around for weeks, inviting people to come and listen to the new Beatles songs: 'They'll be out in four weeks, but why wait?' Of course, in those days anything new by The Beatles was as exciting as if someone had discovered an Eleventh Commandment, so I was king-popular for a while.

I can also claim to have been the first DJ to play *Strawberry Fields Forever*. It arrived on the Radio London boat amid great secrecy and was rushed into the studio where I was prattling on. Gingerly, I put it on the turntable and played it to the audience, listening to it myself and thinking: 'What? This isn't like a pop song, it's like an experience!!' It certainly was one of the weirdest records ever made. After playing it, I put the needle back on and heard it again, trying to fathom out what it was all about. Couldn't then, can't now; but still my firm fave.

I went to the Abbey Road recording studios once to interview The Beatles and they were all feeling very up and playful so the interview went well. Except when I tried to talk to John.

'So, John,' I said. 'How's it going?'

'Oh, a lot of brown paper bags, Ken.'

'Ah. Good. Yes. And how's the album coming along?'

'Yes. Lots of stuff in bags.'

'Good. Fine. Right then. Er, Paul. . . .'

But apart from that the interview went well and they ended up fiddling around with their guitars and pianos and doing a bunch of jingles for me and Radio One. Not bad, huh, having **The Beatles** do your jingles?

I came across **Yoko** a couple of times. The first time was at John's house in Weybridge. Lee and I had gone down to do an interview for the BBC and Yoko was just getting over a bout of 'flu, but when we arrived she got out of bed and cooked us a nut cutlet, which was quite a friendly thing to do. She sat there knitting and talking to Lee while I did the interview, and when I'd finished she said:

'Did you know that men used to do the knitting in the old days? They used to make the sails for their ships.'

What do you say to that? I said something dynamic like 'Oh,' and we left.

A few years ago I got a phone call.

'Hello, this is Yoko.'

'Yoko who?' I inquired. Well, it could have been Yoko O'Reilly, or any number of Yokos.

Anyway, it turned out that she and John wanted to send a message to the newspapers of the world. They didn't want to do any interviews, but obviously they were besieged day and night by requests from the world's Press. They'd decided just to issue a statement and they wanted my help. Instead of paying for yards of advertising space in order to get their message across, they wanted me to call all the newspaper editors and alert them that a momentous message was on its way from John and Yoko.

I did as I was asked and was surprised when the newspaper people said that they wanted to read it first. I'd thought they'd leap at the chance to publish the labels on John's socks. I called Yoko back and told her that the papers wouldn't print The Statement sight unseen. So she sent me a copy that I could circulate to the Press.

When I read it I could see why the editors had been cautious. It was a statement about where she and John 'were at' and didn't make any sense to me. The end of the statement was something like: 'Even as we are writing this, there are three angels watching over our left shoulder.' Your average docker would not think much of that, I thought, but I rang a friend at *The Observer* and read The Statement over the phone.

There was a long silence. He'd fallen asleep. When he woke up he said he couldn't publish any of it, because it was drivel and made no sense at all. I sent him the complete spiel anyway, because that's what Yoko had asked me to do, and a couple of weeks later *The Observer* ran an item in their Pendennis column, tearing The Statement to pieces and quoting all the most laughable bits. So instead of the reception they'd hoped for, John and Yoko wound up looking like a couple of nellies.

It was a strange episode. If they'd wanted to send a message to the world so that everyone would leave them alone, they should have done something that was comprehensible. But the message they sent was so obscure, it only provoked more questions about what they meant.

It was obviously a shock when the news came through that John had been murdered, but I didn't get as worked up about it as most people. Having met the guy a few times, I figured that his philosophy would have prepared him for whatever was going to happen next. I think he would have decided: 'Oh well, obviously this bit's over, so I'm off to the next. See ya. Whoever's-In-Charge has other plans for me at the moment, so it's time to go somewhere else.' We should just be grateful that he did so much while he was here. I'm glad he was in the mood to write all those great songs and talented enough to trim them down and polish them up into wonderful material that will be around forever.

It's not as if he was only halfway through and hadn't produced his best work yet. There were a couple of good tracks on his last album, *Double Fantasy*, but I don't think anyone could reasonably expect him to keep churning out classics. He'd done his bit, and that was that.

I met **Marc Bolan** about a week before he died. I was doing an interview programme on Capital and he came in for a chat; the only problem was that he'd brought a girl with him and all he wanted to do was plug her record. He wasn't interested in talking about himself, which was quite refreshing but not why we'd asked him in. He kept trying to steer the conversation around to this girl's song, and I kept moving him away from it because I hadn't heard it, and it's not wise to play anything on the radio before you've heard it. As the interview progressed he got more and more insistent that we should play the record and then he got quite ferocious. His eyeballs began to steam and change colour and his speech became erratic and quite insulting.

'I've come in here to plug this record, and all you want to talk about is the same old boring crap. . . .' In the end, when the programme had about thirty seconds to go I had to cut him off in mid-sentence which made him even more livid, and he stormed off without so much as a goodbye.

Do you remember *Juke Box Jury*? It was extraordinary, wasn't it? A bunch of people in their nineties all pronouncing judgment on the latest fab tunes with sentences like: 'Well, it's OK, I suppose, if you like that sort of thing. The problem is that you can't hear what they're singing.' In those days, of course, the lyrics were the last thing we worried about – as long as a record had a good tune, it was OK by us, right gang?

I was on *JBJ* once . . . only by the skin of my teeth. I'd wandered out of the studio to buy a packet of winegums and I got lost on the way back to Television Centre. Then I got lost inside, and I arrived in my street clothes on the set and sank into my chair just as they were announcing my name on the air. The programme was live in those days and I must have given the producer several thousand heart attacks.

I sat on the panel, listening to a bunch of records, and I decided that the programme needed livening up, so I determined to be outrageous and make a name for myself.

'**Engelbert Humperdinck**,' I said, 'should be strung up by his vocal cords and pelted with atomic bombs. The noises he makes are an insult to my earholes.' It wasn't considered hip to like people like Hump in those days, and I was keen to show how groovy I was. My comments provoked a bijou-controversy-ette in the music papers which lasted for several weeks.

Engelbert would say something insulting about me every time he was interviewed, and I'd retaliate the next week in another interview by saying that he should be boiled in minestrone and do the world a favour by not making his terrible records. Years later, when I had mellowed into the tolerant, easy-going, polite little sausage you see before you today, I played one of his records, *Les Bicyclettes of Belsize*, and said: 'I used to say dreadful things about that man, when I was young and in my salad days. But he's a sweetie really, and made some good tunes in his time.'

The next day, a telegram arrived. 'Thanks Ken, that was nice. Hump.'

It's funny what you do when you're young, just to get on. I'm sure that all my naughty outrageousness in the early days was just a ploy to get me noticed. I didn't plan it that way in a calculating manner, because I simply wasn't clever enough to think of something so devious. But as I got more and more attention every time I did something slightly naughty, it seemed to be a wise policy to pursue in the getting-on stakes.

I used to admire **Elvis Presley** a lot in the early days, when he was making good, hard-rock tunes like *Hound Dog* and *Blue Suede Shoes*. But the stuff he was doing in the last years of his life was terrible and had no soul. He suffered from the factory-machine approach of those around him, who pushed him in various directions with bigger and bigger cheques instead of letting him stay the great rock and roller he was at the beginning.

I think he's better off in heaven. He was definitely in a trap with no way out, and he obviously couldn't go on forever dressing up like a great big ninny in white spangly suits and playing to a bunch of rich oiks in Las Vegas. What did that have to do with the young sex-symbol everyone used to love?

Just after he died, the air was thick with tributes to Elvis, but I think Radio Moscow said the best thing of all when they pointed out that he'd been scooped up by a bunch of self-seeking capitalist monsters who just wanted to make a big and quick buck and weren't interested in anything else. That's the first and last sensible viewpoint ever aired by Radio Moscow

There were lots of looney people around in the Sixites, all doing daft things. **Dusty Springfield** is a lovely lady and we were quite matey with her. Her only trouble was that she was a bit of a drama queen and was always threatening to commit suicide. We'd often get calls saying that she was about to do it, and so we'd rush round with Band Aid and stomach-pumps at the ready and discover her sitting in bed just looking pale.

It's not something to be taken lightly, when people threaten to do themselves in, but after the ninety-sixth false alarm, we suggested she had zips inserted into her wrists. People who cry wolf a lot will probably outlast the lot of us. They'll scare us all into having heart attacks.

I used to bump into **Cilla Black** quite often at parties. She's one of those great hardy show-business perennials. She hasn't had a hit in years, but she garnered so much goodwill during the time she was at her peak that it will probably keep her in popularity until she's in her wheelchair.

Cilla had a flat opposite Broadcasting House and I could see her window from the studio I used to do the shows from. I was playing one of her records on the radio one day and I suddenly saw this frantic figure in the opposite building, leaning out of her window and waving madly in my direction. I was about to alert an ambulance to a potential suicide bid, when I realized it was just Cilla Black waving to say thanks for playing my tune. Sweet girl.

Hot Gossip have now become household names, like Rentokil. Although we gave them the big break on TV, it was Mary Whitehouse who really helped them on their way to stardom. She saw them on one of the early shows and issued a proclamation from her mountain of moral majorityness that they were obscene and should be wiped from the face of the earth. The Press loved that, of course, and Hot Gossip became instant celebrities.

I couldn't understand what she was making so much fuss about. I mean, they were only lovely bodies writhing about, which is what bodies are for, isn't it? After you've done all the basics with your body, all the things you need to do to stay alive like working and filling them full of food, what's left but to have a good writhe?

The publicity that we got through the meanderings and silly grievances of one blue-rinsed old lady was worth thousands of pounds. Every time reporters called her about something, they seemed to throw in a question about Hot Gossip, and she was forced finally to say: 'I think we've given them quite enough publicity.' Thank you, Mary, from the bottom of our bank balances.

Here's a good test to decide whether or not you side with her or with us purveyors of harmless fun. Who would you rather be stuck in a lift with – Mary Whitehouse or Hot Gossip? Answers on a postcard, please. . . .

I remember once when the Hot Gossipers were smoking a naughty cigarette in their dressing-room: one of the Thames executives walked past and caught a whiff of the fumes. He stormed around the building screaming: 'Out, they've got to get out!!'

We all tried to soothe him and explain that we could hardly fire them because they were one of the main attractions of the show. 'No, no,' he said. 'I don't want to fire them. Just get them out of the building. The police would shut us down if they caught them at it.'

So the boys and girls, all dressed in their skimpiest, naughtiest costumes, had to file outside into the street, stub out the joint in the gutter and then file back inside, like a pack of mischievous schoolkids.

There is a man somewhere who is blessed with the most spectacularly lucky gift imaginable to mankind: he is a **Kenny Everett Look-a-like**. I've never actually met him myself, but he wrote to my agent informing her of the glad tidings and she arranged to meet him and promptly forgot about it. A few weeks later a man walked into her office. She looked up from a sheaf of papers and said: 'Hello, love. Didn't expect you, pour yourself a drink. I'll be finished with this in a moment.'

The man did as she said and sat waiting for her to complete her paperwork. 'Now then, Ev,' she said eventually, 'what can I do for you?' Of course, it wasn't me at all, but my double who, according to Jo who has never been known to exaggerate (well, not until at least the twelfth brandy), was as close to being me as it is possible to be without having been born in Liverpool and suffered the ravages of time.

I'm not sure that I'd like to come face to face with him, wherever he is but, if you read this, Sir, you have my deepest sympathy. I'll keep my bank balance, you can have the sympathy. OK?

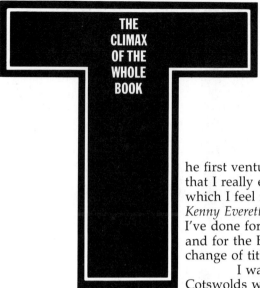

he first venture into television that I really enjoyed, and of which I feel rather proud, is the *Kenny Everett Video Show* which I've done for Thames Television and for the BBC with a slight change of title.

I was living in the Cotswolds when the invitation to do the Thames show came in a telephone call from Philip Jones, Head-Of-Fun-Things at Thames Television. The conversation went something like this:

Me: 'Yes, dammit, now what is it?'

PJ: 'Er, terribly sorry to bother you, Your Aubergineness. My name is Philip Jones and I'd like you to do a TV show for Thames, starring you, with anything you'd like in it. We will, of course, pay you a vast amount of money for the privilege of using Your Extreme Wackiness on the tube.'

Me: 'Not today, thanks.'

Well, maybe it wasn't exactly like that, word for word, but you get the general gist. I really didn't want to do any television work. My forays into that world had been less than successful and I was quite happy loafing about in the Cotswolds. A week later he called again and offered even larger cheques, but I still wasn't that keen because doing weekend shows for Capital while living the existence of a country squire-ette was keeping me and my bank balance quite healthy. Another week passed, and there was another phone call offering even more money. Again, I said no. The fourth offer was irresistibly irresistible and I couldn't resist it. I caved in under the weight of zeros.

I was a bit apprehensive, but I went to London for a meeting with David Mallett who had directed lots of videos and was generally considered to be the second most talented human being alive (after Britt Ekland, that is). David and I had much the same ideas about the sorts of sketches and styles we wanted to try out. He also raved about a new dance group he'd heard of, which didn't thrill me because I'd only seen Pan's People and *Come Dancing* and the whole idea of a dance troupe in the middle of a comedy show seemed a bit daft . . . until I saw the members of Hot Gossip in writhing, sweating, leather-bound, undulating action.

The show was built around a very strict policy which it took hours of formula-making meetings to arrive at. Each show would consist of silly bits, daft bits, outrageous bits and looney bits: a winning combination, we thought. David suggested two scriptwriters, Barry Cryer and Ray Cameron, from whose lips flow witticisms of the like not heard since Wally Whyton wrote scripts for Marcel Marceau.

Barry and Ray are two absolute gems who feed me with great lines such as

This chapter illustrated by Malcolm Harrison.

'Pass the salt' and 'Good evening' and I was endeared instantly to Ray, himself formerly a comedian, by a story he told of a time when he'd been booked to do a big cabaret act in a snazzy nightclub in Australia. The place sounded very posh and as though it would attract a sophisticated clientele, so he decided to polish up his act to make it razor sharp, bought a suit to match and went along to the club. As soon as he walked in the door he thought: 'Forget the high-class material – I need all the tit and bum jokes I can remember.' This was because the first thing he saw as he walked into the lobby was a glass cage, containing a live mouse. Underneath the cage was a big sign which said: '$1,000 to the first person to eat this mouse!'

Barry and Ray are stalwarts and have come to my rescue time after time when the little red light goes on and the audience is slavering and panting after great gags. My mind almost invariably goes blank and I am heard to screech: 'Cryer, peel me a gag!' and either he or Ray toss a golden line into my ear which is regurgitated a few moments later from my mouth in front of the audience.

We don't do the telly shows in front of a live studio audience. We use the camera crew and studio technicians as our audience, which in a way is more difficult because they've heard everything, and there's no 'show-biz' magic attached to the whole caboodle as far as they're concerned. We do have a small ploy to guarantee laughs from the crew, however: we buy large rounds of drinks after the show, which they forfeit if they don't roll about in hysterics every time I draw breath.

We've since moved from Thames to the BBC but the set-up is much the same. It's impossible to sit down at a desk and come up with consistently funny ideas for sketches and gags, and a lot of the ideas first see the light of day when we're nattering in the car on the way to the studio, or when the three of us get together for lunch. One or the other of us will say something which will spark off a train of thought in the others and suddenly a chance remark becomes a thirty-second sketch. Laughter produces laughter and from the three of us joking about something we've seen, heard or done, the basics for a routine are formed and it's then just a case of embroidering and polishing the initial idea.

Tell you what, I've got to go to lunch with Barry and Ray now, so I'll tape-record the whole thing and we'll see what happens.

The scene: The Trattoo Restaurant in Kensington, London. The following are snippets of conversation, uttered in between mouthfuls of fettuccine and large gulps of Bloody Mary. A friend of mine, Simon, came along to referee.

Barry: Bleughcrughpth! (He's taken a large gulp of fettuccine by mistake.)

Ray: It's no good, the script girl will never be able to spell that.

Barry: Pass the parmesan.

Ray: I like working this way. It's nice to take the odd day off to be able to take stock of what's going on.

Barry: I'm normally the lazy one who likes to take days off. It's nice to have a slightly less frenetic schedule and to be able to relax, isn't it?

Ray: No. (Laughter from me and BC.)

Barry: Well, this is a day off in real terms, isn't it?

Me: That's something that never used to be said, isn't it? 'In real terms.' A phrase is born.

Barry: You realize, of course, that you are the one replaceable element of the show.

Me: Me?

Barry: Yeah, we write every single word of every single sketch. You're just a mouthpiece for our gems. An ego-maniac, a prima donna and hell to be with. But, that apart, there *is* a black side to you.

Ray: Don't flatter him Barry, you know what he's like.

Me: Who?

Barry: You.

Me: Oh.

Barry: I had an idea this morning . . . scribbled it on my fag packet (fumbles in pocket). Ah yes (reads) 'Consulate', oh, that's the brand. Well, I had an idea anyway.

Me: Most of our ideas come out of conversation. . . .

Barry: And watching other people's shows.

Ray: Yesterday's lunch came up with three ideas. I don't remember them now, but it was fun thinking of them. Oh yeah, the folding chair man at the BBC: the Head of Folding Chairs.

Me: Mmmmm? What was the gag?

Ray: There's no gag yet.

Barry: We want it to grow organically.

Ray: Then there was the mini-serial. And the dinner party conversation about jealousy (laughs uproariously at memory of previous day's lunch conversation; gets no response from others; wilts).

Barry: This will be the last series, won't it?

Ray: I thought the *last* series was the last series.

Simon: How was Marcel Wave conceived? (Marcel Wave is a camp French philanderer character on the telly shows, just in case you've lived this long without seeing him.)

Me: He was around long before we came along . . . at least the phrase was.

Barry: Yes, it was a hairstyle. They mentioned it in *Some Like It Hot:* 'I'm going home early to marcel wave my hair,' or something like that.

Me: What was it?

Barry: It was a sort of twist. . . .

Ray: It was a Frenchman with a false chin.

Barry: You wore him on your head. Actually we introduced him because there were a lot of randy jokes around and we needed a vehicle.

Ray: Yeah, we needed a vehicle in order to get away with a lot of old randy jokes. And Sid Snot (another character, dressed in black leather and festering with unspeakable habits) has been used in a lot of impressionists' acts.

Barry: I'm all for that, it's just when they pinch the jokes as well that I get riled.

Me: What would make you *not* mind if someone nicked your joke?

Ray: Money.

Barry: Yes, money. Or enormous admiration for the person who nicked it. It's flattering if someone very good steals a joke.

Simon: And what about Gizzard Puke?

Ray: He was invented out of necessity. We thought we couldn't take Sid with us from Thames to the BBC. . . .

Barry: We had a solicitor's letter because the *Radio Times* had printed Grizzard instead of Gizzard and a very respectable Leeds family with the name Grizzard were insistant that we shouldn't use the name, or anything sounding remotely like it.

Barry: But Gizzard is in the dictionary, so there wasn't much they could do. The BBC sent back a wonderful broadside letter quoting the Oxford Dictionary which explains that gizzard is a secondary stomach. . . .

Me: And then they did 'puke', just in case there was any complaint about that. They prefaced the letter with something like: 'This may not be the most savoury letter you've ever received but. . . .'

Simon: The last show, incidentally, was the best thing on TV in ages.

Ray: Thank you. Do you mean you're not paying the bill?

Simon: Did you get any complaints about the sketches?

Barry: No . . . well, one or two phone calls.

Ray: It's only cranks that complain. Actually, the Beeb said they'd had a whole Niagara Falls of complaints about a sketch we did called 'Shoot The Dog' which was a mickey-take of those ghastly American quiz shows where people do things like eating sideboards if the prizes are high enough. 'Shoot The Dog' was the logical extension to that where the contestants are confronted by the cutest, fluffiest little dog you can imagine and Ev as Master of Ceremonies tempts them with more and more money, willing them to give in and let their greed overtake their scruples.

Me: Their what?

Ray: Scruples.

Me: Never heard of them.

Barry: That comes as no great surprise.

Ray: Anyway, the Beeb told me they had a torrent of complaints about 'Shoot The Dog'. 'How many?' I asked. 'Well, at least a dozen,' they said. But there are 12 million people out there, for Chrissakes . . . if you only offend one millionth of your audience, you're doing pretty well in my book.

Barry: Absolutely. God alone knows how many people are offended by Val Doonican. Why don't they have a go at him and leave us alone?

Ray: But to be fair, the BBC generally puts on more adventurous shows than ITV – Python, Alf Garnett, TW3, Not the Nine O'Clock News, OTT. . . .

Me: That's ITV, not the Beeb.

Ray: Don't quibble when I'm proving a point. The biggest challenge at the BBC is finding your way around everything in time to come up with a programme at the end of the red tape and Departments of Everything-You-Could-Possibly-Think-Of.

Barry: It's a cross between the army and a school.

Ray: Hey, I didn't tell you the quicksand joke, did I?

Barry: Yes.

Ray: Oh.

Simon: Do you like watching the programme once you've spent hours and weeks putting it together, or can't you bear to watch the finished product?

Me: It's fun watching the good bits.

Barry: I like watching it the second time. The first time I see it, I'm too busy nit-picking with myself about things that weren't quite right and worrying about what's coming up next – will it be any good? The second time I can relax and look for the sketches and bits I really liked. When I've seen it three hundred and sixty-eight times, I normally switch off and congratulate myself on a good show. Eric Morecambe sits and watches his shows back and laughs and laughs – tears coursing down his cheeks. It's quite endearing really, not so much a case of 'Aren't I great' as 'Isn't *he* funny.'

Ray: What's exciting about our shows is that Ev doesn't read things until the last minute. I'll write a piece with Barry and say to you: 'Do you want to see it?' You'll say 'No' and only see it moments before you do it to camera – it really is exciting. Fresh and lively. Whether it's funny or not is another matter.

Me: I also find it much easier to do re-takes nowadays.

Ray: You're getting more and more professional all the time.

Barry: Relaxed. Much more relaxed.

Ray: Yes. Professional is not the word. Relaxed is more like it.

Me: You mean sloppy.

Ray: Did I say sloppy? No, it's more as though you're more confident and not so keen to get things over with as quickly as possible.

(At this point the conversation veered towards politics. A heated debate ensued and rapidly died down again when it became apparent that none of the participants had the foggiest idea what they were talking about.)

Barry: We've almost finished lunch and we haven't come up with a single idea for a sketch yet.

Ray (to waiter): I'll have a Coca-Cola, please.

Barry: What we need is something hysterically funny and clever.

Me: Mmmm. Would make a change.

Ray: What we need is a real Whooooph! of an idea.

Simon: What's a Whooooph!?

Me: It's a shorthand way of indicating massive audience appreciation: mega-applause!

Ray: Yeah. It's fantastic to hear those laughs. We screened the Xmas show to an audience at the Shepherd's Bush Theatre so that we could add real laughter and the reaction was great. Up until then, we'd only told ourselves that they liked it out there.

Me: They even laughed at things that we didn't think were funny. A great bonus.

Simon: Who does the warm-up for the audience?

Me: Me. Barry does the pre-warm-up warm-up. . . .

Ray: Then Kenny went on and said 'fuck' three or four hundred times. . . .

Barry: Just to break the ice you understand. . . .

Ray: Then he picked up a Christmas tree and hurled it like a javelin into the audience, and it hurtled through the air, my mind went into slow motion and I had this image of the tree going right into an old man's eye: suing time!

Barry: I can just imagine the conversation: 'I got Kenny Everett's autograph.' 'You got his autograph, so what? He killed my father!'

(Simon is eating his way through a bowl of mussels and suddenly goes green.)

Me: Problems? (pointing to plate of empty mussel shells).

Simon: I think they're off. I may have discovered too late, having just eaten nine-tenths of them.

Barry: Your plate looks like an explosion at Sidney Opera House.

Me: How about introducing an Australian character into the show?

Barry: Yeah, we talked about that but you can't avoid Dame Edna or Les Patterson. Barry Humphries has covered every antipodean possibility with just those two characters.

Me: But if we had a character who looked very, very different. . . .

Ray: The attitude would be the same: it's either Les or Edna.

Barry: Let's invent a new character, here and now.

Ray: We toyed with an Arab.

Barry: No need to rake up old skeletons while we're trying to come up with ideas.

Ray: I think we're on to a winner with our new character, Cupid Stunt.

Barry: Only problem is that the BBC fainted at the thought of that name going out on television, so she's euphemistically being referred to as Cupid Start.

Ray: That's the BBC closing their ranks, military-style, and putting their foot down.

Barry: 'Do what you like,' they say. But suddenly they think you've gone just a bit too far and there's a teeny slap of the wrist and they say: 'No, that's what she's called, all right? Off you go and be good boys.' They said it very nicely, but there was no mistaking that they meant business. They're very firm on those areas of policy, and it doesn't really matter in terms of the show.

Ray: That's not really how the name changed. They called up and said: 'Could you change the name?' and we said: 'How much?'

Barry: So we called her Mary Hinge, instead.

Me: Is there something funny behind that?

Barry: It's a spoonerism.

(I'm in full coffee-slurp when I cotton on to the Mary Hinge joke and Barry ducks to avoid the spray that gushes from my mouth along with gales of laughter.)

Barry: The hundreds of times I've said 'Mary Hinge' to you and you've only just got it. . . .

Me: I was just thinking of Hinge itself being a funny name. . . .

Barry: Everyone latches on to Cupid Stunt fairly quickly, but Mary Hinge is a slightly more subtle version.

Waiter: Coffee?

Barry: Do you have cappuccino?

Waiter: Si.

Me: What's the one in the little cup? The gravelly, butch, dark one?

Barry: Charles Bronson.

Waiter: You mean espresso, signor?

Me: That's the one.

Simon: Of all the star guests there have been on the show, have any of them been pains in the ass, or were they all sweet and delightful?

Me: Pains in the ass never actually made it onto the studio floor. They would just get a bit hoity-toity on the phone when discussing an idea for a sketch and say things like: 'Oh, I'm not doing that sort of thing: I'll look ridiculous,' so we'd just say: 'Forget it' and find someone who didn't mind doing silly things for a laugh.

Barry: Adam Ant was a bit cool. It wasn't our idea to have him in the first place. His entourage made it known that Adam would be happy to appear on the show, so we wrote him into a sketch and when we came to record it, this insipid-looking person arrived and declared that he didn't want to wear the make-up. I had to bite my lip and try not to say: 'If you don't wear the make-up, who's going to know who the hell you are?' Then we were told by the managers that he wouldn't do a sketch in jeans. 'Adam doesn't wear jeans,' they said. Crazy! It's just like a sketch in itself – the star who won't wear jeans! Apart from that one silly episode, we've been very lucky with people on the show. I think we've developed a kind of instinct about who would and who wouldn't be good for the show.

Ray: We had a good night a while ago when we crammed a load of people into the Comedy Store and filmed a gaggle of comics doing stand-up routines to a live audience. *The Kenny Everett Juke Box*, it's called, and the finished product is selling like hot cakes.

Barry: Too bad it's not selling like video cassettes.

Me: We don't seem to have produced many ideas for the show yet.

Ray: This kid is not slow off the mark. Pour him another brandy.

(A short discussion followed on the subject of Lennie Bennett, comedian and game-show host.)

Me: He paid one of the all-time great backhanded compliments to me once. We were chatting about Steve Martin, an American comedian who, in my opinion, is the funniest man in the world. 'Steve Martin?' said Lennie. 'He's not funny at all. *You're* funnier than he is.' Silver-tongued devil.

Ray: Let's stop slagging people off. Let's talk about great people. Let's talk about *us*.

Me: But we haven't got any ideas for the show. . . .

Barry: Have another brandy.

Simon: How do you decide on whether or not to do a sketch. Is the criterion, if it makes you laugh, it works?

Me: Broadly speaking, yes.

Barry: No. The criterion is, if it makes us laugh, we do it. If it works, we get a bonus. But there is seriously no better way to work things out. It all boils down to us in the finish. There is no such thing as a 'them' that we're aiming at. There's no real barometer of what is funny and what isn't.

Ray: And that's where you get a conflict with the people who run whichever company you're working for, Thames, the BBC . . . whoever . . . because they're concerned with what They think people want to see. . . .

Barry: We are, do you realize, probably the only programme ever to write sketches for and make use of every orifice in the human body.

Ray: Oh, yeah, we had that aerosol which cleaned up bad language.

Me: Then there was the Hootermatic – the vacuum cleaner for your nose.

Barry: And Fragro-pan . . . a kind of personal Harpic.

Ray: And Pimple-On. That was my favourite. A whole buiid-up spiel about acne, pimples, spots . . . the whole caboodle and then . . . 'Don't you miss them? Well, Pimple-On can bring back memories of the good old spotty teenage days.' (Assembled company breaks up laughing at memory of Pimple-On sketch.)

Simon: It all sounds like too much fun. It's hardly work, is it?

Barry: Oh, it's work all right, but it's keeping the fun going that is the trick. If you're trying to create fun in an atmosphere where fun is stifled, it simply won't work.

Ray: It's also the last-minuteness of Ev's involvement that helps too . . . he arrives breathless, just before we're due to do a take, grabs the script, has a quick read-through and goes straight in front of the camera . . . that's where the magic is.

Simon: Is that a deliberate policy, or is it just laziness?

Me: Mostly laziness.

Barry: No it's not. It's an instinctive understanding of your modus operandi.

Me: It's an instinctive understanding of my modus operandi.

Ray: We're beginning to script your entire life!

Me: They're beginning to script my entire life!

Ray: I'll tell you, one of my favourite days on the show was one day when we got into the studio early one morning . . . a mistake. I hasten to add, it won't happen again . . . anyway, Barry and I were sitting in the office and we got an idea to try out a kind of Mary Whitehouse character who would have balloons for tits which would burst at the end of the sketch. We dragged a passing costume designer in and said: 'If there's any time at the end of the day's schedule, we'd love to try this idea. Is there any chance of knocking up a costume between now and the end of the session?' Off he went and we carried on with the pre-arranged line-up of work and at the end of the day there was about an hour left, so Ev went off to clamber into this new, hastily knocked-up costume. While he was changing, we wrote three or four jokes and he came back from the wardrobe department with about fifteen minutes of studio time left and no time to read the gags we'd written. The lines were typed up onto the Auto-Cue, on went the lights, the cameras turned and he just did it: no rehearsal, no read-through, just On. And it was magic. I must say I've never been so impressed. . . .

Me: Before or since. . . .

Ray: Yeah, at the time it was great. Now everything you do looks exactly like that instant character. Come to think of it, Angry of Mayfair was born in that same last-minute way. It obviously pays off.

Simon: Do you work to any kind of set formula as to the length of each sketch or item?

Ray: Ah, yes. We have a very strict policy on that issue. The content of the TV shows are divided into three categories: short bits, medium bits and long bits.

Barry: Call us old fashioned if you like, but it seems to work.

Ray: On average we get through about thirty bits on each show. On ITV, a half-hour programme is actually only twenty-four and a half minutes when you take into account the ads. On the Beeb, a half-hour is a half-hour is a half-hour, which means a lot of extra writing. In fact a BBC series of thirteen weeks is actually the same in terms of consuming material as a Thames series of fifteen weeks. (A thought strikes him). We're not getting enough money!

Simon: Do you ever disagree about whether or not a joke or a sketch is funny, or do you work by committee?

Ray: We seldom disagree on what's funny and what isn't. On the occasions that we have differed, it's probably because a joke isn't right in the first place, so we just scrap it . . . unless it was *my* idea, in which case I bring out a Sherman tank in order to prove my point. They're very accommodating when faced with brute strength.

Me: Anyone want to come and help me choose a gas cooker?

Barry: I would consider it the crowning glory of my career.

Me: Well, we haven't come up with any ideas for the show yet.

Barry: The night is young, dear boy. Have another brandy.

Me: I hate brandy.

Barry: Nonsense. Waiter, more brandies please.

So there you are, dear reader, a privileged glimpse of three of the mightiest brains in television today, hard at work in the endless, fearless search for new, boundary-stretching material that will rock the nation to its socks.

ENDISPIECE

Well, darling reader, I can feel the back
cover getting closer and closer so I guess
that's about all there is to say
for the moment. Pity, really, because things are just
beginning to get interesting but,
as you can see, we're running out of paper and I've
never been one to outstay my welcome.
If you're ever passing, you will drop in, won't you?
There now, you've promised.
Until we meet again, I'll just leave you
with this thought:

Yours until the heavens turn into a side-street . . .